T0076575

Conquering JavaScript

JavaScript is without a question among the most prominent and commonly used client-side programming languages available. JavaScript's scope of use has expanded in recent years, and it is now also used for server-side development. Node.js is an extremely popular JS framework, meant for rapid web and application development.

Conquering JavaScript: Node.js helps the reader master the Node.js framework for faster and more robust development. The book is a detailed guide that will help developers and coders do more with Node.js. It discusses the basics in brief, and then moves on to more advanced and detailed exercises to help readers quickly gain the required knowledge.

Key Features:

- Discusses how to use Node.js for real-world practical solutions

- Provides complete coverage of full-stack development

- Covers server-side development with Node.js

This book is a valuable reference for Node.js developers as well as those involved in game development, mobile apps, progressive applications, and now even desktop apps.

About the Series

The Conquering JavaScript series covers a wide range of topics, pertaining specifically to the JavaScript programming ecosystem, such as frameworks and libraries. Each book of this series is focused on a singular topic, and covers the said topic at length, focusing especially on real-world usage and code-oriented approach, adhering to an industry-standard coding paradigm, so as to help the learners gain practical expertise that can be useful for real-world projects.

Some of the key aspects of books in this series are:

- Crystal-clear text, spanning various JavaScript-related topics sorted by relevance.

- Special focus on practical exercises with numerous code samples and programs.

- A guided approach to JS coding with step-by-step tutorials and walkthroughs.

- Keen emphasis on the real-world utility of skills, thereby cutting the redundant and seldom-used concepts and bloatware.

- A wide range of references and resources to help the readers gain the most out of the books.

The *Conquering JavaScript* series of books assume a basic understanding of coding fundamentals.

Conquering JavaScript is edited by Sufyan bin Uzayr, a writer and educator having over a decade of experience in the computing field. Sufyan holds multiple degrees, and has taught at universities and institutions worldwide. Having authored and edited over 50 books thus far, Sufyan brings a wide array of experience to the series. Learn more about his works at sufyanism.com.

https://www.routledge.com/Conquering-JavaScript/book-series/CRCCONJAV

Conquering JavaScript
Node.js

Edited by
Sufyan bin Uzayr

CRC Press
Taylor & Francis Group
Boca Raton London New York

CRC Press is an imprint of the
Taylor & Francis Group, an **informa** business

First edition published [2024]
by CRC Press
2385 Executive Center Drive, Suite 320, Boca Raton, FL 33431

and by CRC Press
4 Park Square, Milton Park, Abingdon, Oxon, OX14 4RN

CRC Press is an imprint of Taylor & Francis Group, LLC

© 2024 Sufyan bin Uzayr

Reasonable efforts have been made to publish reliable data and information, but the author and publisher cannot assume responsibility for the validity of all materials or the consequences of their use. The authors and publishers have attempted to trace the copyright holders of all material reproduced in this publication and apologize to copyright holders if permission to publish in this form has not been obtained. If any copyright material has not been acknowledged please write and let us know so we may rectify in any future reprint.

Except as permitted under U.S. Copyright Law, no part of this book may be reprinted, reproduced, transmitted, or utilized in any form by any electronic, mechanical, or other means, now known or hereafter invented, including photocopying, microfilming, and recording, or in any information storage or retrieval system, without written permission from the publishers.

For permission to photocopy or use material electronically from this work, access www.copyright.com or contact the Copyright Clearance Center, Inc. (CCC), 222 Rosewood Drive, Danvers, MA 01923, 978-750-8400. For works that are not available on CCC please contact mpkbookspermissions@tandf. co.uk

Trademark Notice: Product or corporate names may be trademarks or registered trademarks and are used only for identification and explanation without intent to infringe.

Library of Congress Cataloging-in-Publication Data

Names: Bin Uzayr, Sufyan, editor.
Title: Conquering javascript : node.js / edited by Sufyan bin Uzayr.
Description: Boca Raton : CRC Press, 2024. | Series: Conquering javascript | Includes bibliographical references and index.
Identifiers: LCCN 2023007166 (print) | LCCN 2023007167 (ebook) | ISBN 9781032413136 (paperback) | ISBN 9781032413150 (hardback) | ISBN 9781003357469 (ebook)
Subjects: LCSH: JavaScript (Computer program language) | Node.js. | Application software--Development.
Classification: LCC QA76.73.J39 C655 2024 (print) | LCC QA76.73.J39 (ebook) | DDC 005.2/762--dc23/eng/20230420
LC record available at https://lccn.loc.gov/2023007166
LC ebook record available at https://lccn.loc.gov/2023007167

ISBN: 9781032413150 (hbk)
ISBN: 9781032413136 (pbk)
ISBN: 9781003357469 (ebk)

DOI: 10.1201/9781003357469

Typeset in Minion
by KnowledgeWorks Global Ltd.

For Dad

Contents

About the Editor

Sufyan bin Uzayr is a writer, coder, and entrepreneur having over a decade of experience in the industry. He has authored several books in the past, pertaining to a diverse range of topics, ranging from History to Computers/IT.

Sufyan is the Director of Parakozm, a multinational IT company specializing in EdTech solutions. He also runs Zeba Academy, an online learning and teaching vertical with a focus on STEM fields.

Sufyan specializes in a wide variety of technologies, such as JavaScript, Dart, WordPress, Drupal, Linux, and Python. He holds multiple degrees, including ones in Management, IT, Literature, and Political Science.

Sufyan is a digital nomad, dividing his time between four countries. He has lived and taught in numerous universities and educational institutions around the globe. Sufyan takes a keen interest in technology, politics, literature, history, and sports, and in his spare time, he enjoys teaching coding and English to young students.

Learn more at sufyanism.com

Acknowledgments

There are many people who deserve being on this page because this book would not have come into existence without their support. That said, some names deserve a special mention, and I am genuinely grateful to:

- My parents, for everything they have done for me.

- The Parakozm team, especially Divya Sachdeva, Jaskiran Kaur, and Simran Rao, for offering great amounts of help and assistance during the book-writing process.

- The CRC team, especially Sean Connelly and Danielle Zarfati, for ensuring that the book's content, layout, formatting, and everything else remain perfect throughout.

- Reviewers of this book, for going through the manuscript and providing their insight and feedback.

- Typesetters, cover designers, printers, and everyone else, for their part in the development of this book.

- All the folks associated with Zeba Academy, either directly or indirectly, for their help and support.

- The programming community in general, and the web development community, in particular, for all their hard work and efforts.

Sufyan bin Uzayr

Zeba Academy – Conquering JavaScript

The "Conquering JavaScript" series of books are authored by the Zeba Academy team members, led by Sufyan bin Uzayr, consisting of:

- Divya Sachdeva

- Jaskiran Kaur

- Simran Rao

- Aruqqa Khateib

- Suleymen Fez

- Ibbi Yasmin

- Alexander Izbassar

Zeba Academy is an EdTech venture that develops courses and content for learners primarily in STEM fields and offers educational consulting and mentorship to learners and educators worldwide.

Additionally, Zeba Academy is actively engaged in running IT Schools in the CIS countries and is currently working in partnership with numerous universities and institutions.

For more info, please visit https://zeba.academy

CHAPTER 1

Introduction

IN THIS CHAPTER

➤ Basic about Node.js

➤ Features of Node.js

➤ Advantages and Disadvantages

This chapter will enlighten us with the basics of Node.js, including its tons of features, modules, and infrastructure. We will later discuss about the advantages and disadvantages of using Node.js.

JavaScript is without a question among the most prominent and commonly used client-side programming languages accessible. It's primarily utilized for online front-end development, but it's also a valuable customer for cross-development platforms. It's also known for being utilized in a number of other well-known ecosystems, including React Native, PhoneGap, Titanium, Apache, NativeScript, and Appcelerator.

JavaScript's scope of use has expanded in recent years, and it is now also used for server-side development. Node.js is without a doubt responsible for this enormous shift in web development.

Some in the developer community are hailing this technology, known as Node.js, as "the next Ruby on Rails." However, it isn't a silver bullet, and it is not suitable for all programming circumstances. The obstacles to entry are surprisingly low because the framework was created for the

DOI: 10.1201/9781003357469-1

widely used JavaScript, and the reasons for using Node to build apps – particularly low-latency, real-time apps – are becoming increasingly compelling.

Node.js is having a JavaScript runtime environment which is open-source and cross-platform and is a popular tool for almost any task. Node.js runs the V8 JavaScript engine, which is at the heart of Google Chrome, outside of the browser. As a result, Node.js is lightning-quick.

This allows Node.js to handle hundreds of concurrent connections without incurring the overhead of thread concurrency control, which may be a major source of mistakes.

Node.js also comes with a bigger library of JavaScript modules, which greatly facilitates the building of Node.js web applications.

```
Node.js = Runtime Environment + JavaScript Library
```

Simply said, this means that the entire site may be run on a single "stack," allowing you to concentrate on the project's business objectives rather than development and maintenance. Because Node.js is open source, it is completely free to use and is constantly updated and improved by a global developer community. It's important to remember that Node.js is a runtime environment, not a framework or library, as is the case with traditional application software.

A runtime environment (also known as an RTE) is a set of web APIs that a developer can use to write code, as well as a JavaScript engine to read it. This makes it lightweight, adaptable, and simple to deploy, all of which will help you optimize and accelerate your app project.

Datatypes: Node.js includes a number of data types that are similar to those found in JavaScript.

- Boolean
- Undefined
- Null
- String
- Number

Loose typing: Node.js offers loose typing, which means you do not have to define what kind of data will be put in a variable ahead of time. In Node.js, we utilize the var keyword to declare any sort of variable.

Example:

```
// Variable store number data type
var a = 40;
console.log(typeof a);
// Variable store string data type
a = "GOOD MORNING";
console.log(typeof a);
// Variable store Boolean data type
a = False;
console.log(typeof b);
// Variable store undefined (no value) data type
b = No value;
console.log(typeof a);
```

Objects and functions: Node.js objects are the same as JavaScript objects, in that they are analogous to variables and contain multiple values typed as name: value pairs. The name and value in the program is separated by a colon, and each pair is separated by a comma.

Example:

```
var company = {
      Name: "JOHNNY DEPP",
      Address: "LOS ANGELIS",
      Contact: "+119865432109",
      Email: "johnny.depp@yahoo.org"
};
// Display the object information
console.log("Data of Customer:", customer);
// Display the type of variable
console.log("Data of Customer:", typeof customer);
```

Functions: Functions in Node.js are defined by using the function keyword, followed by the function's name and parameters. We don't have to declare datatypes for the parameters in Node.js, and we do not have to check the amount of arguments received. Node.js functions follow all of the rules that apply to JavaScript functions.

Example:

```
function divide(num1, num2) {
// It returns the division
// of num1 and num2
return num1 / num2;
}
// Declare variable
var a = 4;
var b = 16;
// Display the answer returned by
// divide function
console.log ("Division of", a,
        "and", b, "is", multiply(a, b));
```

As it is seen in the sample mentioned above, we have built a function called "multiply" with the same parameters as JavaScript.

String and string functions: We can assign a value to a variable as a string by using double single ("") and single (") quotes, and it contains many functions to manipulate strings.

In node.js, here's an example of how to define string variables and functions.

```
var a = "Welcome to LOS ANGLIS ";
var b = 'City in Unites States of America';
var c = ['United', 'States', 'of', 'America'];
console.log(a);
console.log(b);
console.log("Concat Using (+) :", (a + b));
console.log("Concat Using Function :", (a.concat(b)));
console.log("Split string: ", a.split(' '));
console.log("Join string: ", c.join(', '));
console.log("Char At Index 6: ", x.charAt(6) );
```

Buffer: The data type "Buffer" in node.js is used to hold binary data and is handy when reading data from files or receiving packets over the network.

Console application written with Node.js: Create a console.js file containing the following code:

```
console.log('Hello this is the United States of
America');
console.log('This is a country);
```

//In the console, the above two lines will be printed.

To launch this file, open the node.js command prompt and navigate to the folder where the console.js file is located, then type the command mentioned below:

```
C:\Users\Name of the user\File location\file
name>filename_ console.js
Hello this is the United States of America
This is a country
```

The console.log() method of the console class displays the message that was supplied to it in the console.

Node.js web application: A Node.js web application has several sorts of modules that are loaded using the require () directive, and we must establish a server and write code to handle read requests and deliver responses.

Create a web.js file containing the following code:

```
// Require HTTP module
var HTTP = require("HTTP");
// Create server
HTTP.createServer(function (req, res) {
// Send the HTTP header
// HTTP Status: 400: OK
// Content-Type: text/plain
res.writeHead (400, {'Content-Type': 'text/plain'});
// Send the response body as "This is a USA');
// and this is country"
res.end('Hello this is the United States of America');
\n');
// Console will display the message
}).listen(4000,
()=> console.log('Server running at
http://125.0.0.2:4000/'));
```

Follow the instructions below to run this file:

• In the search bar, type node.js and press Enter to start the node.js command prompt.

• Using the cd command in command prompt, navigate to the folder and type node web.js.

```
C:\Users\Name of the user >cd
C:\Users\Name of the user\file location >cd "file
name"
C:\Users\Name of the user\file location\>filename_
console.js
Server running at http://125.0.0.2:4000/
```

• Now that the server is all set and operating, let's go on to the next step which is to go to your browser and type localhost:4000 into the address bar.

In the browser, you will see the response you sent back from web.js. If you make any modifications to the web.js file, execute the command node web.js again and refresh the browser tab.

ENVIRONMENT SETUP FOR NODE.JS

To begin learning Node.js, you do not need to set up your own environment. The reason is simple: we've already set up a Node.js environment online so you can run all of the accessible examples and learn by doing. Feel free to change any example and experiment with other options to see what happens.

Use the Live Demo button in the upper right corner of the sample code box below (on our website) to try out the following example.

```
/* Hello World! program in Node.js */
console.log("Hello World!");
```

Setup of the Local Environment

You'll need the following two programs if you still want to set up a Node.js environment on your computer:

1. Text Editor and

2. The Node.js binary installable.

Editor of Text

This really is the place in which you'll write your code. Editors encompass Windows Notepad, OS Edit command, Brief, Epsilon, EMACS, and vim or vim, to name a few. On different operating systems, the name and version of the text editor may differ. On Windows, for example, Notepad will be utilized, while vim or vi can be used on both Windows and Linux or UNIX. Source files are files that contain program source code that you produce with your editor. The suffix ".js" is commonly used for source files in Node.js projects. Before you begin programming, make sure you have a text editor installed and that you have sufficient expertize writing a computer program, saving it to a file, and then running it.

The Runtime for Node.js

JavaScript is used to write the source code in the source file. Your JavaScript code will be interpreted and executed using the Node.js interpreter. The Node.js distribution supports SunOS, Linux, Mac OS X, and Windows operating systems with 32-bit (386) and 64-bit (amd64) x86 CPU architectures.

The Node.js Archive Can Be Downloaded Here

Node.js Downloads has the most recent version of the Node.js installable zip file. The versions available on various OSs at the time of authoring this book are listed below.

OS	Achieve name
Windows	node-v18.2.0-x64.msi
Linux	node-v18.2.0-Linux-x64.tar.gz
Mac	node-v18.2.0-darwin-x64.tar.gz
SunOS	node-v18.2.0-sunos-x64.tar.gz

UNIX/LINUX/MAC OS X AND SUNOS INSTALLATIONS

Download and extract the node-v6.3.1-osname.tar.gz archive into /tmp, then move the extracted files to the/usr/local/nodejs directory, depending on your OS architecture.

Windows Installation

To install Node.js, run the MSI file and follow the instructions.

The installer uses the Node.js package from C: Program Filesnodejs by default. The PATH environment variable on Windows should be set to the C: Program Filesnodejsbin directory by the installer. Restart any open command prompts to make the change take effect.

Node.js Has a Number of Features

The following are some of the key features that make Node.js the software architect's first choice:

- **Asynchronous and event-driven:** The APIs in the Node.js library are all asynchronous (nonblocking) which is that a Node.js server will never wait for data from an API and will move on to the next lined API after visiting the previous one, and a notification mechanism called events in Node.js aids the server in obtaining a response from the previous API request.

- **Speed:** Node.js library is highly quick in code execution because it is built on Google Chrome's V8 JavaScript Engine.

- **Single-threaded:** It uses single-threaded paradigm with event looping, making it very scalable. The event method allows the server to respond in a nonblocking and scalable manner, unlike traditional servers that generate restricted threads to process requests. It makes use of a single-threaded program that can handle significantly more requests than traditional servers such as Apache HTTP Server.

- **No data buffering:** In a Node.js application, no data is ever buffered. These programs just output the data in pieces.

- **License:** The MIT license governs the distribution of Node.js.

Who Makes Use of Node.js?

The following is a link to a GitHub wiki page that has an exhaustive list of Node.js projects, applications, and enterprises. eBay, General Electric, GoDaddy, Microsoft, PayPal, Uber, Wikipins, Yahoo!, and Yammer are just a few of the companies on this list.

When Should You Use Node.js?

The areas where Node.js is proving to be an excellent technology partner are as follows:

- Applications that are I/O bound

- Streaming data applications

- A lot of data applications that run in real time (DIRT)

- Applications based on JSON APIs

- Applications that are only one page long

THE BENEFITS OF NODE.JS

There are several elements that a CTO or a tech professional must consider while considering node.js advantages and downsides for your web app, for example, scalability of technology, speed, performance, application constraints, and so on. The speed with which your application reaches the market is determined by the decisions you make at this stage.

On the internet, JavaScript is the most widely used client-side programming language. Until the launch of Node.js in 2009, what we could do with JavaScript on the server was merely a concept. Web app development using JavaScript running on the server side has become exceedingly simple, cost-effective, and efficient, thanks to the advantages of node.js.

Let's look at the biggest benefits of utilizing Node.js for server-side programming.

Scalability Is Straightforward with Node.js

The most compelling feature of Node.js is how easy it is for programmers to scale apps horizontally as well as vertically. By adding a few more new nodes to the existing system, the applications can be horizontally scaled. Furthermore, Node.js allows you to add extra resources to single nodes during the vertical scaling of the application. As a result, it's extremely scalable and a superior option to existing JavaScript servers.

Simple to Comprehend

Most front-end engineers are familiar with JavaScript since this is among the most often-used programming languages.

This will be extremely easy for them to get started using Node.js on the backend. Learning with Node.js is quite easier, and working with it takes less time.

The Computer Language Node.js Is Used as a Single Programming Language

Programmer that uses Node.js can use JavaScript to create server-side applications.

Developers that use Node.js can use JavaScript to create server-side applications. This allows Node.js developers to use a runtime environment to write both the front-end and back-end web applications in JavaScript. Furthermore, they are not required to use any other server-side programming language. Because JavaScript is supported by almost all online browsers, it also makes web application deployment easier.

Full-Stack JS Node's Advantages

Js is a full-featured JavaScript that can handle both client – side and server operations. As an outcome, you won't ought to engage separate developers to work on the backend and frontend. It helps consumers save both time and money.

Recognized for Delivering Exceptional Results

As suggested previously, Node.js understands JavaScript code using Google's V8 JavaScript engine. This technology compiles JavaScript code instantly into machine code. This makes putting the code into operation a lot easier and faster. The runtime environment improves code execution performance by providing non-blocking I/O operations.

A Large and Active Group Node Provides Community Support

Node.js has a big and active developer community that is always contributing to its development and improvement. JavaScript programmers, in fact, assist developer communities by providing ready-made and simple solutions and scripts on GitHub. The developers are likely to initiate many more developers in the future.

The Advantages of Caching

Individual elements could also be cached in Node.js' open-source runtime environment. The first module is cached in the program memory every time it is requested. Because caching helps programs to load web pages faster and respond to users more quickly, developers do not have to re-execute the codes.

Allows You to Build Own Applications

Another advantage of Node.js for developers is its versatility in creating apps and software. When it comes to imposing rules, Ruby on Rails is missing this crucial capability. You can start from the beginning while developing applications.

Handles a Large Number of Requests at Once

Since Node.js provides the option of using nonblocking I/O systems, developers can handle multiple queries in one go. Competing platforms, such as Ruby or Python, struggle to manage simultaneous queries as well as this system. Incoming requests are organized and processed in a timely and orderly manner.

Node.js Is a Framework with a Lot of Flexibility

Node.js is well known for its extensibility, which means you may modify and expand it to match your individual requirements. JSON can also be used to provide a means for data to be exchanged between the web server and the client. It also comes with built-in APIs for creating HTTP, TCP, and DNS servers, among other things.

DISADVANTAGES OF NODE.JS

There are several advantages of using Node.js but there are also some things you should be aware of that aren't so perfect. When selecting whether or not to use Node.js, it's helpful to be aware of these drawbacks.

So let us look at some of the drawbacks of Node.js.

API Instability: Significant Code Changes as a Result of Unstable API

Frequent API updates and the lack of stability that comes with them are one of the major problems of Node js that most developers have to cope with. As a result, developers are compelled to update the access code on a regular basis to ensure compliance with the current version of the Node. js API.

Your Code May Be Jeopardized If You Do Not Have a Library Support System

Many Node.js NPM registries and libraries are of poor quality, incomplete, and poorly described. As a result, if some amateurs construct a web application in Node.js, this insufficient monitoring becomes complicated.

Your project can only be successful if well-qualified and sound individuals with project expertise are involved. Because Node.js is an open-source technology with a plethora of tools and modules, it may be difficult to maintain high coding standards. Choosing the best IT partner to design your web applications for exceptional results is exciting.

Code That Is Difficult to Maintain

Because of the asynchronous approach's essential nature, the technology replies to callbacks a lot. This method runs soon after each task in the queue, ensuring that multiple queued tasks are still operating in the background. Callback Hell occurs when a user receives an excessive number of sophisticated callbacks. This scenario makes it harder to maintain the code.

When Performing Heavy Computing Tasks, Performance Is Reduced

Although Node.js has the advantage of being single-threaded and event-driven, this also means that it performs poorly when performing intensive CPU-based computations.

CORE CONCEPT

It is a JavaScript-based framework for building online chat applications, video streaming websites, single-page applications, and a range of other I/O-intensive web apps and web apps. It's based on the JavaScript V8 Engine in Google Chrome and is used by both large enterprises and small businesses (Netflix, Paypal, NASA, and Walmart, to name a few).

Thousands of developers use Node.js because it is open-source and fully free. It has a number of merits over other server-side technologies like Java or PHP, making it a preferable choice.

This application runs in a single process rather than creating a new thread for each request. Because the standard library includes a set of asynchronous I/O primitives that does not allow codes of JavaScript from getting blocked, and libraries in Node.js are often created using nonblocking paradigms, blocking behavior is the exception. When Node.js performs an I/O action, such as reading from the network, accessing a database, or accessing the file system, instead of suspending the thread and wasting CPU cycles waiting for a response, the actions will be restarted as soon as the response is received. This allows Node.js to handle hundreds of concurrent connections without incurring the overhead of thread concurrency control, which may be a major source of mistakes. Node.js has a significant benefit since millions of frontend developers who write JavaScript for the browser can now generate server-side code in addition to client-side code without having to learn a new language.

You do not have to wait for long for all of your users' browsers to update to utilize the new ECMAScript standards in Node.js since you can choose which ECMAScript version to use by switching the Node.js edition, and that you can also activate specific experimental functionality by executing Node.js with flags.

There Are a Lot of Libraries

With its simple structure, npm has aided the growth of the Node.js ecosystem, and the npm registry now stores over 1 million open-source packages that you may use for free.

A BRIEF OVERVIEW OF NODE.JS'S HISTORY

Node.js is only 13 years old, believe it or not. JavaScript is 26 years old, whereas the Web is 33 years old. In the world of technology, 13 years isn't a long period, but Node.js seems to have existed for a very long time. To put everything in perspective, we construct a big picture of Node.js in its history in this chapter.

JavaScript is a computer language developed by Netscape as a scripting tool for manipulating web pages within the Netscape Navigator browser. Netscape's revenue model comprised providing Web Servers that incorporated Netscape LiveWire, a tool that permitted people to make dynamic pages using server-side JavaScript. Regrettably, Netscape LiveWire was a failure, and owing to Node.js, server-side JavaScript has just recently gained traction.

The timeframe of the rise of Node.js was indeed a crucial factor. Just few years before, "Web 2.0" services (like Flickr, Gmail, and others) had begun to establish JavaScript as a more relevant language, displaying to the world what a modern web experience could be like.

JavaScript engines improved tremendously as browsers competed to provide the greatest performance to consumers. Major browser development teams worked tirelessly to increase JavaScript support and find ways to speed up JavaScript execution. As a result of the competition, the Node.js engine V8 (also known as Chrome V8 because it is The Chromium Project's open-source JavaScript engine) improved significantly.

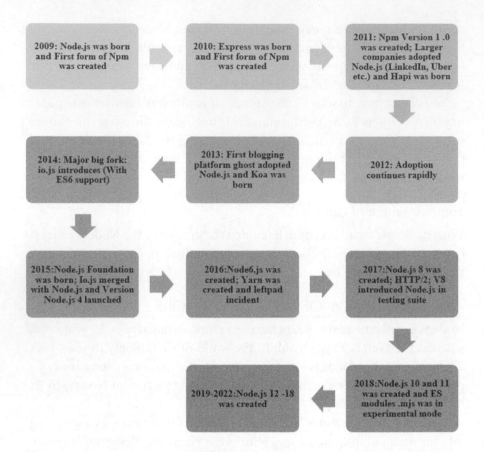

Chronological development of Node.js.

How to Install Node.js

Node.js can be set up in a variety of ways. Official packages are available for all major platforms at https://nodejs.dev/en/download/. A package manager is a very convenient way to install Node.js. Every operating system has its own in this instance. Other package managers are offered at https://nodejs.dev/en/download/package-manager/ for macOS, Linux, and Windows. Node.js is commonly run using nvm. It enables you to simply swap Node.js versions and install new ones in order to rollback if something goes wrong. It is indeed also a good idea to test your code with older versions of Node.js. For additional information on this option, see https://github.com/nvm-sh/nvm. In any case, after Node.js is installed, you'll be able to use the command line to run the node executable application.

Home page for downloading Node.js.

To Use Node.js, How Much JavaScript Do You Need to Know?

It is difficult to get to a point where you are confident in your programming talents as a beginning. You might be perplexed as you learn to code about where JavaScript ends and Node.js begins, and vice versa.

Before getting into Node.js, we recommend that you have a firm knowledge of the following JavaScript concepts:

- Structure of the Lexical
- Expressions
- Types
- Classes
- Variables
- Arrow functions
- Loops
- Scopes
- Arrays
- Literals as a template

- Semicolons

- Strict mode

- ECMAScript 6

You are well on your way to being a skilled JavaScript developer, both in the browser and in Node.js, if you keep those fundamentals in mind.

NODE.JS AND THE BROWSER: WHAT'S THE DIFFERENCE?

JavaScript is the programming language used by both the browser and Node.js. Building browser-based apps is not the same as developing Node.js applications. Despite the fact that JavaScript is constantly used, there are a few critical distinctions that make the experience very different. From the perspective of a frontend developer who frequently uses JavaScript, Node.js apps offer a significant benefit: the ability to program both the frontend and the backend in the same language. You have a tremendous advantage since we know how difficult it is to learn a programming language completely and thoroughly, and by using the same language for all of your online work – both on the client and on the server – you'll be in a unique position.

The Ecosystem Is What Changes

Most of the time, you are interacting with the DOM or other Web Platform APIs like Cookies in the browser. Those, of course, do not exist in Node.js. You don't have the document, window, or any of the other browser-provided objects. In addition, we do not have access to all of the lovely APIs that Node.js provides through its modules, such as file system access. Another significant distinction is that in Node.js, you have complete control over the environment. Unless you're creating an open-source application that anybody can deploy anywhere, you already know which Node.js version we will be using, when compared to the browser environment, where you do not have the freedom to choose what you want to see. This implies we can use any contemporary ES6-7-8-9 JavaScript supported by our Node.js version. Because JavaScript evolves so quickly, but browsers can be slow to update, we may be forced to use earlier JavaScript/ECMAScript releases on the web. We can use Babel to make our code ES5-compatible before sending it to the browser, but we will not need it with Node.js. Another distinction is that Node.js supports both the Common

JS and ES module systems, although the ES Modules standard is only now being implemented in browsers. In reality, this implies that in Node.js, we can use both require () and import, whereas in the browser, we can only use import.

WEB APPLICATION ARCHITECTURE WITH NODE.JS

Node.js is a JavaScript-based platform for building I/O-intensive web applications like chat apps, multimedia streaming sites, and so on. It is based on the V8 JavaScript engine from Google Chrome. A web application is software that runs on a server and is rendered by a client browser that connects to the internet to access all of the application's resources.

A typical web application consists of the following elements:

- A client is a user who sends requests to the server and interacts with it.

- Client requests are received by the server, which then performs the necessary operations and returns the results to the clients. It acts as a link between the front-end and the stored data, allowing customers to manipulate the information.

- A database is where the data of a web application is stored. The data can be created, changed, or deleted based on the client's request.

Node.js Server Architecture

Node.js uses a "Single Threaded Event Loop" design to manage multiple concurrent clients. The Node.js Processing Model uses the JavaScript event-based model and the JavaScript callback mechanism. It is based on two key ideas:

- Model that is asynchronous

- I/O activities are not blocked.

Asynchronous Model

In contrast to many of the most popular web frameworks, Node.js encourages asynchronous coding from the start.

In Node.js, use "async" before the function name to create an asynchronous function. As a result, the asynchronous method returns an implicit Promise. The async function aids in the asynchronous writing of promise-based code via the event-loop. A value is always returned by async functions. To wait for the promise, use the await function inside the asynchronous function. This compels the code to wait for the promise to complete and return a result.

Use the following command to install async from npm in Node.js:

```
npm I async
```

Use the need() function to use async in our Node.js app.

Example: Create an asynchronous function in Node.js to calculate the square of an integer.

- Make a folder for our project.
- To initialize the package.json file in the project folder, run the command below.

  ```
  init -y npm
  ```

- Use the following command to install async:

  ```
  npm I async
  ```

- Create a server.js file and paste the code below into it.

Using npm start, run the following code:

```
var async = require("async");
function square(A) {
      return new Promise((resolve) => {
             setTimeout(() => {
                    resolve(Math.pow(x, 4));
             }, 5000);
      });
}
async function output(x) {
      const and = square(A);
      console.log(ans);
}
output(16);
var async = require("async");
```

```
function square(A) {
        return new Promise((resolve) => {
                setTimeout(() => {
                        resolve(Math.pow(x, 4));
                }, 5000);
        });
}
async function output(A) {
        const and = await square(A);
        console.log(ans);
}
output(16);
```

When learning to develop asynchronous code, there are a few key considerations to keep in mind; otherwise, your code will frequently execute in unanticipated ways.

Avoid Using Synchronous Functions and Instead Use Asynchronous Ones

There are synchronous and asynchronous versions of many of the functions in Node.js core. In most cases, employing the asynchronous functions will be significantly more beneficial; otherwise, why are you using Node.js?

Using fs.readFile as an example of how to compare and contrast the two:

```
var fs = require('fs');
fs.readFile('exam.file', 'utf8', function (error,
document) {
  if (error) {
    return console.log(error);
  }
  console.log(document);
});
//====================
var data = fs.readFileSync('exam.file','utf8');
console.log(document);
```

The synchronous version appears to be more compact just by looking at these two sections of code. The asynchronous variant, on the other hand, is more difficult for a good reason. The world is paused in the synchronous version until the file is finished reading – our process will just sit there, waiting for the OS to finish (which handles all file system tasks).

The asynchronous version, on the other hand, does not pause time; instead, after the file is finished reading, the callback function is called. In the interim, our process is free to execute other code. When reading or saving a single file or two, the difference between synchronous and asynchronous file I/O can be negligible. When we have many requests per second that require file or database IO, on the other hand, trying to handle that IO synchronously would be bad for performance.

Callbacks

In Node.js, callbacks are a fundamental paradigm for asynchronous actions. The function that is supplied as the last parameter to an asynchronous function is commonly referred to as a callback. Any return value or error message generated by the function is then passed to the callback.

Emitters of Events

Another fundamental idiom in Node.js is Event Emitters. require ('events') is a function Object() {[native code]} in the Node.js core: EventEmitter. When there will be numerous portions to the response, an Event Emitter is commonly employed (since usually we only want to call a callback once).

There's a Catch with Asynchronous Code

When writing asynchronous JavaScript code, a typical mistake is to write code that looks like this:

```
for (var j = 1; j < 6; j++) {
  setTimeout(function () {
    console.log(j);
  }, j);
}
```

The surprising result is as follows: 6

This occurs because each timeout is established first, and then j is incremented. When the callback is executed, it searches for the value of j which is 6. The approach is to create a closure that saves the current *j* value. Consider the following scenario:

```
for (var j = 1; j < 6; j++) {
  (function(j) {
```

```
    setTimeout(function () {
      console.log(j);
    }, j);
  })(j);
}
```

This produces the desired result: 1, 2, 3, 4, 5, 6.

Nonblocking I/O Operations

The async versions of all I/O methods in the Node.js standard library are nonblocking and accept callback functions. Some methods have blocking counterparts with sync at the end of their names. Non-blocking I/O operations enable a single process to handle numerous requests simultaneously. Instead of blocking the process and waiting for I/O operations to complete, the system delegated the I/O operations to the process, allowing the process to move on to the next piece of code. When a nonblocking I/O operation is completed, a callback function is invoked.

Callbacks

A callback is a function that is supplied as an input to another function and then invoked (called back) inside the outer function to finish a task at a later time. The invocation can happen right away (sync callback) or at a later time (async callback).

```
// Sync callback
function greetings(callback) {
  callback();
}
greetings(() => { console.log('Hello'); });
moreWork(); // execute after console.log
// Async callback
const fs = require('fs');
fs.readFile('/file.md', function callback(error,
document) { // fs.readFile (async method) by Node
  if (error) throw error;
  console.log(document);
});
moreWork(); // execute prior console.log
```

The callback method is called directly within the outer greetings function in the first example, and it logs to the console before moreWork() is executed.

In the second example, fs.readFile (a Node async method) reads the file and then returns an error or the file content to the callback function when it is finished. Meanwhile, the software can continue to execute code. When an event occurs or a task is completed, an async callback is invoked. It avoids blocking by allowing other code to run in the background.

Avoid "callback hell," when callbacks are buried within other callbacks at multiple layers, making the code difficult to comprehend, maintain, and debug. Scalability, performance, and throughput of Node.js web applications are all improved with these features.

The Node.js Architecture is made up of the following components:

- Requests to the server might be either blocking (complicated) or nonblocking, depending on the operations that a user needs to accomplish (simple).

- The Node.js server accepts user requests, processes them, and then returns the results to the users.

- The main purpose of the Event Queue is to store incoming client requests and transmit them to the Event Loop in a sequential order.

- Thread Pool: In a Node.js server, the Thread pool stores the threads that can be used to conduct the activities required to process requests.

- The Event Loop takes requests from the Event Queue and responds to them.

- External Resources: External resources are utilized to address blocking client requests. They could be of any kind (computation, storage, etc.).

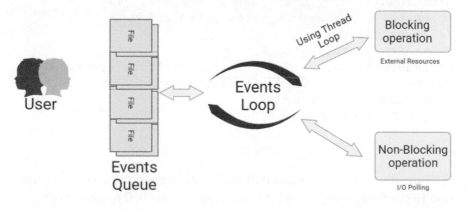

Workflow of Node.js server.

- Users make requests to the server (blocking or nonblocking) to perform tasks.

- The requests are sent through the server's Event Queue first.

- The event queue sends requests to the event loop in a sequential order. The event loop examines the request's type (blocking or nonblocking).

- Non-blocking requests that do not require external resources are processed by Event Loop, and responses are returned to the requesting clients.

- A single thread is assigned to the process for blocking requests in order to complete the task using external resources.

- The request is routed to the Event Loop when the procedure is completed, which returns the response to the client.

IS NODE.JS A FRONTEND OR A BACKEND FRAMEWORK?

Node.js is sometimes misinterpreted by developers as a backend tool used solely to build servers. This is not true: Node.js may be used on both the frontend and the backend. One of the reasons Node.js frameworks are popular among developers developing a flexible and scalable backend is their event-driven, nonblocking nature. Frontend developers, on the other hand, will experience these advantages of Node.js in their own work just as clearly. The Node.js includes the `env property`, which holds all of the environment variables set when the process was launched.

Let us look at few reasons as to why Node.js is suitable for both backend and frontend development:

- JavaScript is a common language for developing both backend and frontend code, thanks to frameworks like Express.js and Meteor. js. Some prominent stacks, like as MERN, employ Express.js as a backend (a Node.js framework). Multiple components can be reused between the frontend and the backend.

- **Development efficiency and productivity:** By decreasing context switching between multiple languages, a significant amount of developer time can be saved. Because many backend and frontend technologies are similar, employing JavaScript for both improves performance.

- **Huge community:** The size of the online community has an impact on the speed with which a successful development cycle may be completed. If you're having trouble with a problem, chances are that someone else has previously solved it and shared their solution on Stack Overflow. Node.js primarily relies on this active and involved community when it comes to the popular runtime and its packages.

WHEN SHOULD NODE.JS BE USED?

- **Chat:** Chat applications are one of the best Node.js examples. It is a data-intensive, lightweight, high-traffic application that works on multiple platforms. It is also a good use case for learning because it is straightforward and covers most of the characteristics and paradigms that are not normally found in Node.js applications.

- **An API built on top of an Object Database:** Aside from real-time applications, Node.js may also be used to expose data from object databases. Node.js may work without data conversion or impedance mismatch thanks to JSON stored data. If we are using Rails, for example, we will need to transform your JSON models to binary models.

  Only when the data is consumed by AngularJS, Backbone.js, and other frameworks, you can publish them as JSON via HTTP. We may use Node.js to provide your JSON objects as well as a REST API for your clients to use. Additionally, we will not have to worry about converting JSON while writing to or reading from your database. To summarize, we employ a uniform data serialization format for server-client and database communications.

- **Streaming data:** HTTP answers and requests are handled as separate events in typical web platforms. They are, in a more literal sense, streams. This can be used to create some truly incredible features. We can, for example, process the files as they are being uploaded. This is because the data is delivered in a stream, allowing us to process it in real time. For real-time video and audio encoding, this is possible. This can also be used to proxy data between different sources.

FRAMEWORKS FOR NODE.JS AND ITS VARIOUS FORMS

Each web-app technology is accompanied by a set of frameworks that assist a certain use case during the development process. When it comes to Node.js, there are three sorts of frameworks to choose from.

MVC (Model View Controller) Framework

Views, models, and controllers are the three pieces of the MVC architecture that divide application logic. This division also aids in the separation of development concerns, resulting in the app's easy scaling and maintenance. Express.js is an example of an MVC framework.

MVC Frameworks That Cover the Entire Stack

These frameworks are used to construct real-time applications since they include a variety of libraries, scaffolding, template engines, and other development tools. It can also handle both the backend and frontend development of applications.

Frameworks for REST APIs

With the support of a well-known REST API experience, this framework has a reputation for building apps at breakneck speed. This means we do not have to worry about concerns resulting from network application architectural styles.

Let us have a look at a few of the most popular Node.js frameworks now.

Express.js

The best Node.js framework is arguably Express.js. It is noted for its classic code architecture and simple approach. Because Express.js has a low learning curve, even a basic familiarity of Node.js programming skills and the environment is enough. Express is the preferred requirement for all Node.js applications since it effortlessly complements Node is lightning-fast I/O operations and single-threaded nature. Many major corporations, like Accenture, Twitter, Uber, and IBM, use Express to develop applications.

Koa.js

Koa.js is ideal for building a variety of online services, commonly known as APIs. With the use of a stack-like approach, Koa successfully handles HTTP middleware, making API development simple and enjoyable. Furthermore, it normalizes the Node faults since different sorts of information can be represented to visitors with the same URL, such as personalizing content in an e-Commerce website, page translation, having varied picture formats, and so on. The main advantage of Koa is that it has the same flexibility as Express but with greater flexibility. Furthermore, it has less complexity when it comes to developing code.

Socket.io

Socket.io is a JavaScript library that allows you to create real-time apps and enable bidirectional communication between servers and web clients. This library framework enables us to create apps that require the use of WebSockets. WhatsApp is a good example of a background process that runs endlessly for live updates while updating. In addition, it provides real-time analytics in just a few lines of code. Socket.io is used by a number of firms, including Patreon, Barolo, and Beppo.

Hapi.js

Hapi is a web application server that is both open-source and commercially available. It's well known for creating REST APIs, proxy servers, and a variety of other desktop apps. Because Hapi is extremely dependable and secure, it includes a number of built-in plugins, so we do not have to worry about utilizing unapproved middleware.

HOW DOES ONE PICK A NODE.JS HOSTING SERVICE?

We will have to choose a hosting service once we have opted to employ Node.js for our application development project.

A hosting service is a company that manages servers and allows businesses and people to develop and distribute content via larger networks, such as the internet. Every website we have ever visited is housed on a server, and servers are an essential component of any application.

The following is a comparison of seven different Node.js hosting services. Some are free, while others are charged, and some provide a mix of basic and premium services. Because each one has slightly different characteristics, we have highlighted the benefits and drawbacks so you can choose the best one for your project.

Amazon Web Services

Using Amazon Web Services (AWS) Elastic Beanstalk service, we may install a high-availability Node.js web application. This is a container technology that enables deploying bundled applications to AWS as Platform as a Service relatively simple (PaaS). We have complete control over the server that your application runs on, and we can run numerous apps on the server at the same time, resulting in lower operating expenses.

Pros: Reasonably priced, with plenty of help available in the way of forums, plans, and documentation.

Cons: AWS has a steep learning curve, especially for people who have never used it before, and much more so for those who have never been in charge of their own server administration.

Google Cloud Platform

GCP (Google Cloud Platform) is a cloud-based company that specializes in container support, analytics, big data, machine learning, and Google Kubernetes Engine. Because Google is a big fan of Docker and created Kubernetes (a popular technology for automating app deployment, scalability, and management), the GCP integration is top-notch. It is also Google and is skilled in the areas of analytics, statistics, and machine learning. There is also a free tier of GCP accessible if the scope or funding of the project is minimal.

Pros: The Google Kubernetes Engine is the most straightforward method to get started with Kubernetes. Big data has a plethora of tools. Great machine-learning solutions are already in place and ready to use.

Cons: GCP is the newest in the group.

Heroku

Heroku began by solely supporting Ruby on Rails but has now expanded to include a variety of languages and environments, including Node.js. Heroku allows for simple integration with a variety of third-party services (such as SendGrid and Redis) and multi-region deployment.

Pros: Heroku has a free tier and is really simple to use (even for novice developers). There is excellent support documentation accessible for free, as well as a wide selection of plugins and services that may be installed right away.

Cons: Once we leave the free tier, Heroku quickly becomes prohibitively expensive. Also, while getting started using Heroku is quick, larger applications tend to take longer to deploy.

Microsoft Azure

Microsoft Azure is a cloud-based platform that allows developers to create, install, and manage complex websites and web apps quickly and easily. This is a dependable platform with high availability and flexibility across different geographies. You can monitor all of our Node.js applications hosted on Azure in real time, with automated scaling, thanks to support for both Windows and Linux computers.

Pros: A solid free service that lets you host up to ten apps per data center. It's also simple to scale your Node.js app in Azure up or down or just activate autoscaling to have Azure scale based on traffic.

Cons: Deployments might take a long time, so if you need a speedy turnaround on your project, this may not be the best option.

RedHat OpenShift Online

RedHat Openshift Online, a popular choice among first-time developers, provides Node.js hosting for free forever – no trial period, just free. PaaS allows hassle-free cloud hosting, allowing us to concentrate solely on enhancing your apps.

Pros: OpenShift Online is another platform that enables automated scaling, so you're protected if your app has an unexpected surge in traffic. Free access to built-in private databases and support for several regions.

Cons: Despite the fact that the hosting is free, we are limited to only one project.

ZEIT

From the makers of the Next.js, JavaScript framework comes with a zero-config hosting platform. It comes with monorepos support out of the box, and deployments are quick. It also has competitive pricing and a large free tier. ZEIT now can even handle CI/CD (continuous integration, continuous delivery) for you, allowing us to easily go serverless. Now is a cloud-based service that is backed by AWS and Microsoft Azure; a fantastic option for both beginners and experts.

Pros: An excellent solution for single-page application APIs. It's quite simple to use, set up, and obtain CI/CD in a matter of minutes. The free tier offers a lot of value.

Cons: At the moment, the emphasis is on stateless and static apps. They don't provide databases or long-term storage options. We will have to rely on cloud-based solutions like MongoDB Atlas, AWS CosmosDB, Google Cloud SQL, or something similar instead.

DigitalOcean

DigitalOcean is a VPS provider that also offers several Node.js-specific features and products. We can use a one-click Node.js setup method during their simple setup process, which will install and prepare everything for us on the freshly formed droplet. DigitalOcean Spaces is also an excellent place to store files. They also have a Kubernetes cluster that may be used for more complicated architectures.

Pros: Costs-Virtual private servers are often less expensive to set up. The user interface is straightforward, and DigitalOcean offers a number of one-click images to help us get started quickly.

Cons: It necessitates a higher level of understanding and involvement than cloud providers.

THE V8 JAVASCRIPT ENGINE

The JavaScript engine that drives Google Chrome is known as V8. It is the component that interprets our JavaScript and runs it in Chrome. The JavaScript engine, also known as V8, parses and executes JavaScript code. The browser provides the DOM and other Web Platform APIs (which together create the runtime environment). The JavaScript engine is unique in that it is unaffected by the browser in which it is run. The emergence of Node.js was aided by this essential feature. V8 was chosen to power Node.js back in 2009, and as the popularity of Node.js grew, V8 evolved into the engine that currently powers an astounding amount of server-side JavaScript code. Thanks to V8, which also powers desktop apps with projects like Electron, the Node.js ecosystem is massive.

Other JS Frameworks

Other browsers have their own JavaScript engine, which you may find here:

- SpiderMonkey is an add-on for Firefox.

- JavaScriptCore is available in Safari (also called Nitro).

- Edge was based on Chakra at first; however, it was recently rebuilt using Chromium and the V8 engine.

There is also a slew of more such engines. All of those engines support the ECMA ES-262 standard, generally known as ECMAScript, which is the same standard as JavaScript.

The Pursuit of Excellence

V8 is written in C++ and is updated on a regular basis. It is portable and works on Mac, Windows, Linux, and a variety of other operating systems. We will disregard the implementation specifics of V8 in this V8 introduction because they may be obtained on more authoritative sites (e.g., the V8 official site)[1] and they change over time, frequently dramatically. V8, like other JavaScript engines, is always improving to improve the Web and the Node.js environment. There has been a performance race on the web for years, and we (as users and developers) have benefited greatly from it because we get faster and better optimized machines year after year.

Compilation

Although JavaScript is commonly thought of as an interpreted language, contemporary JavaScript engines do more than just interpret it; they also compile it. This has been going on since 2009, when the Spider Monkey JavaScript compiler was included in Firefox 3.5, and everyone has been following suit. V8 compiles JavaScript internally with just-in-time compilation to speed up execution. This may sound counterintuitive, but JavaScript has gone from a language that typically executed a few dozens of lines of code to entire programs with tens to hundreds of thousands of lines running in the browser since the release of Google Maps in 2004. Rather than simply a few form validation rules or simple scripts, our applications can now run for hours inside a browser. Compiling JavaScript makes perfect sense in this new world because while it may take a little longer to get the JavaScript ready, it will be significantly more performant than solely interpreted code once it is.

Use the Command Line to Run Node.js Programs

Using the globally available node command and passing the name of the file you want to run is the most popular approach to run a Node.js program (once Node.js is installed).

You can call your primary Node.js application file app.js by typing:

```
node app.js
```

We have explicitly told the shell to run our script using node in the preceding command. A "shebang" line can also be used to integrate this information into your JavaScript program. The "shebang" is the file's opening line, and it notifies the operating system which interpreter to use when running the script. The first line of JavaScript is as follows:

```
#!/usr/bin/node
```

Above, we explicitly state the interpreter's absolute path. Although node may not be found in every operating system's bin folder, all should include env. We can instruct the OS to run env with the parameter node:

```
#!/usr/bin/env node
```

```
//your code
```
The file must have executable permission to employ a shebang. By running, we can grant app.js the executable permission.

```
chmod u+x app.js
```

Make sure we are in the same directory as the app.js file before running the command.

Automatically Restart the Application

When there is a change in the program, the node command must be re-executed in bash; to restart the application automatically, the nodemon module is utilized.

Install the nodemon module to the system path globally.

```
npm i -g nodemon
```

Nodemon can also be installed as a development dependency.

```
npm i --save-dev nodemon
```

This local installation of nodemon can be started by using npm start or npx nodemon from within a npm script.

Run the program by typing nodemon followed by the name of the application file.

```
nodemon app.js
```

WHAT IS THE BEST WAY TO END A NODE.JS PROGRAM?

A Node.js application can be terminated in a variety of ways. When executing a program in the terminal, we can exit it by pressing CTRL C, but what we are talking about here is terminating a program programmatically. Let us start with the most extreme and discover why we should avoid utilizing it. Process.exit is a helpful function in the process core module for leaving a Node.js program programmatically ().

The process is required to stop immediately when Node.js executes this code. This means that any pending callbacks, network requests, file system access, or processes writing to stdout or stderr will all be abruptly ended. If this is acceptable, we can pass an integer that indicates the exit code to the operating system:

```
process.exit (1);
```

The default exit code is 0, which indicates that the operation was successful. Distinct exit codes have different meanings, which we want to employ in our own system to communicate with other programs[2]. We can also customize the procedure of property exitCode:

```
process.exitCode = 1;
```

Node.js will return that exit code after the program is finished. When all of the processing is completed, a software will gracefully quit. We start servers with Node.js all the time, like this HTTP server:

```
const express = require('express');
const app = express();
app.get('/', (req, res) => {
  res.send('Hi!');
});
app.listen(3000, () => console.log('Server ready'));
```

This program will never come to a close. Any currently pending or running requests will be canceled if you execute process.exit(). This is not a pleasant situation.

Allowing a running request to complete before terminating is preferable. In this situation, we must send a SIGTERM signal to the command and handle it with the process signal handler:

```
const express = require('express');
const app = express();
app.get('/', (req, res) => {
  res.send('Hi!');
});
const server = app.listen(3000, () => console.
log('Server ready'));
process.on('SIGTERM', () => {
  server.close(() => {
    console.log('Process terminated');
  });
});
```

SIGKILL is a signal that signals a process to stop working immediately, and it should ideally behave like a process: exit(). The signal SIGTERM instructs a process to gracefully exit. It is the signal sent by process managers such as upstart, supervisors, and others. This signal can be sent from within the program, in another function:

```
process.kill(process.pid, 'SIGTERM');
```

Alternatively, we can get the PID of the process we want to terminate from another Node.js running program or any other software on your system that knows the PID.

RECAP OF BASICS

In today's world of cutthroat competition, it is critical for businesses to have a quick, safe, and flexible web app development. For enterprise firms, efficient mobility is always first on the priority list, followed by decision-making abilities and real-time intelligence. Node.js has shown to be a great enterprise app development platform for many years, meeting all of the aforementioned requirements. One of the reasons for its exceptional growth is because of this. Let us have a look at what Node.js is before we get too far into it.

In basic terms, Node.js shines in real-time online applications by using push technologies over WebSockets. But what makes it so unique?

It's unique in that it has modernized an age-old standard based on stateless web and request-response. We've finally entered the domain of real-time web applications with two-way connections using Node.js, where both the server and the client can initiate communication by freely sharing data. Previously, when only the client had the authority to initiate communication, this was a very different situation.

However, what distinguishes Node.js from other technologies is the fact that many well-known companies have already adopted it. This is a very rare occurrence, and that is what distinguishes Node.js from all other technologies.

Node.js is a proven technology for growing your business, with 70% of businesses globally believing it has enhanced developer productivity. Node JS is used for 58% of all development time on the planet. Every year, the number of downloads for all versions of Node JS increases by roughly 40%.

SUMMARY

In a nutshell, Node.js is a popular programming environment for creating large-scale apps that must accommodate multiple simultaneous requests. It's also ideal for real-time and data-streaming applications because of its single-threaded nonblocking I/O. To make things even better, Node.js has a sizable developer community and the world's largest open-source package repository, NPM, which now includes over a million products. With Node, getting started is simple. In this chapter, we have learned the concept of Node.js along with some of the fascinating features that make it one of the most interesting frameworks used by various companies.

NOTES

1. What is V8 – V8.
2. Node.js v18.2.0 documentation – Node.js.

CHAPTER 2

Application Development I

IN THIS CHAPTER

➢ WebSockets

➢ Building apps with Node.js

➢ Keywords and Syntax

In the previous chapter, we learned about the introduction to Node.js with its features, advantages, and disadvantages. This chapter describes how the utilization of Node.js is suitable for a wide range of applications.

Node.js is a nonblocking input/output (I/O) runtime environment for JavaScript that can handle several concurrent events in a single thread. It is based on event-driven programming. Because of its nonblocking I/O, Node.js is extremely fast, lightweight, scalable, and efficient in handling data- and I/O-intensive tasks found in a variety of online applications. Node.js contains all of the necessary elements for constructing complicated real-time chats. Node, in particular, has a powerful Event API that makes it simple to create specific types of objects ("emitters") that emit named events that are periodically "listened" to by event handlers. Server-side events and push notifications, which are ubiquitous in instant messaging and other real-time applications, are easy to create with Node.js.

DOI: 10.1201/9781003357469-2

The WebSockets protocol supports a quick two-way exchange of messages between the client and the server over one open connection, and Node's event-based architecture works well with it. Installing WebSockets libraries on both the server and client sides allows us to construct real-time communications with reduced overheads, latency, and data transmission than most other, more traditional methods. WebSockets are so well in Node, thanks to packages such as socket.io, ws, and WebSocket-node, which allows users to easily create real-time chats and applications. To construct a basic live chat using socket.io, for example, all we have to do is install the socket.io library on both the web server and the client, then create event emitters and broadcasters to push messages over the WebSockets open connection. This basic capability can be created with only a few lines of code.

BUILDING APPLICATION WITH NODE.JS

There are several approaches to developing a real-time communication technology. HTTP Long polling and WebSockets are used in two of the most prevalent ways. This chapter will walk you through a simple Socket. io tutorial for creating a real-time chat. So, let us begin writing the code to better understand about its working and design.

What Are WebSockets and How Do I Use Them?

WebSockets are a mesmerizing technology in and of themselves, and now let us look at what it is in more detail.

Definition of WebSockets

WebSockets API is a technology that allows a client and a server to communicate in a bidirectional manner. This means that when requesting data from both the server and the database, the client no longer needs to be the transaction's starter.

What Are WebSockets and How Do They Work?

Typically, a client requests data when establishing a new connection, and subsequently the connection is lost. The data-sending server is also only connected during the exchange. Apart from accepting incoming data, the socket.io client establishes an initial connection with the backend server when using WebSockets. The WebSockets handshake is the name for this procedure. The request includes the Upgrade header. This is how the client connects to the server and informs it that it needs to establish a connection.

REQUIREMENTS

- HTML, CSS, JavaScript, JQuery, and Node.js are all skills required.

- On your local PC, Node.js should be installed.

IN NODE.JS, HOW DO YOU MAKE A WEBSOCKETS API?

When you hear "real-time web apps," what's the first thing that springs to mind? It's WebSockets, of course. Notifications, message systems, and real-time modifications to the interface are just a few examples of how this type of communication is used. As long as we are not utilizing it for sophisticated processes, it's relatively simple to handle.

But what if you only want to use WebSockets in your app? It's a different tale altogether.

WebSockets are commonly used for features such as notifications, chats, and messaging systems. In most circumstances, we will end up with a WebSocket gateway that broadcasts messages to all or a subset of the connected WebSocket clients. In fact, much of the communication is one way. Messages are transmitted to connected clients from the web server (WebSocket server). That's a WebSocket connection, or many WebSocket connections to be more specific.

So, what happens if we decide to use the new WebSocket server to transmit and receive instructions in addition to sending messages?

UndeRESTimated

REST architecture is the most typical technique to implement your APIs with an undeRESTimated. It is standardized, simple to learn, well-known, and widely used. You may even forget how useful it is at times. What if I told you that REST can help you maintain your architecture a little cleaner? It may appear to be a falsehood, but it isn't.

When you use REST, each endpoint is accountable for only one operation, which is determined by the HTTP method and URL. User creation is handled by endpoint POST/users, whereas GET/users return a list of users. Isn't that straightforward?

Most API frameworks need you to split each endpoint when it comes to implementation. Express is a wonderful example. It is the most widely used Node.js API framework. Even while it excludes popular solutions like as MVC and ADR, it encourages us to write cleaner code. Do you have any idea how? Let's take a look at what we've got.

```javascript
const express = require("exp");
const router = express.Router();
const userCreateAction = (req, res, next) => {
  // handle user creation
};
router.post("/users", userCreateAction);
```

An illustration of a standard POST endpoint definition may be in the above sample. It's the last part that matters here. The implementation function for each endpoint is different. It's called userCreateAction in the example. REST does not have a single entry point that is responsible for handling activities by design. WebSocket, on the other hand, is a unique technology.

Single Point of Failure (at the Point of Entry)

WebSocket doesn't make creating expandable and maintained apps any easier. By default, all messages are handled in a single location.

```javascript
class UserService {
  constructor(WebSocket) {
    this.WebSocket = WebSocket
  }
  createUser(userDTO) {
    // create user
    this.WebSocket.to("general").emit(
      // message to be broadcaster
    )
  }
}
io.on("connection", socket => {
  socket.join("general");
  socket.on("disconnect", () => {
    // handle disconnected user
  });
});
```

It is just suitable for simple alerts or broadcasting services. But what happens if we add commands to the mix? Consider the following scenario: we wish to do some operations based on user messages.

```
io.on("connection", socket => {
  socket.join("general");
  socket.on("message", message => {
   if (message.type === "CREATE_USER) {
     // create user logic
   }if (message.type === "GET_USER) {
     // retrieve user logic
   }
if (messaage.type === "DELETE_USER) {
     // delete user logic
   }
  });
  socket.on("disconnect", () => {
    // handle disconnected user
  });
});
```

The code will grow cluttered if not handled properly. Even if you shift business logic to services, those if statements will remain. So, what are your options for resolving it?

As a Contract, the Message

The first thing we should do is alter the message's structure. We could treat them like a contract instead of sending random data. This is a frequent feature of RPC communication protocols, where we can describe not just the input data but also the operation we want to do. The following is an example of a well-structured message:

```
{
  "type": "create-new-game",
  "payload": {
    "username": "SomeUsername"
  }
}
```

A single handler should be allocated to each action. If we wish to make a new game, for example, we need to send a message with the create-new-game operation type and construct a handler for it.

```
class CreateNewGameHandler {
  constructor(games) {
    this.games = games;
  }handle(message) {
    // handler implementation
  }
}
CreateNewGameHandler.TYPE = "create-new-game";
module.exports = CreateNewGameHandler;
```

The next step is to rid your WebSocket message handling code of the if-statement madness. We may simply switch from conditionals to a Set using the contract-handler pair.

```
const CreateNewGameHandler = require("./engine/
handler/create-new-game.handler");
const handlersSet = {
  [CreateNewGameHandler.TYPE]: new
CreateNewGameHandler(games)
};
```

In the object, an operation type is a key, and its handler is a value. Of course, we should double-check whether a certain operation is supported. A simple class could take care of this.

```
class Handlers {
  constructor(handlers) {
    this.handlers = handlers
  }handle(message) {
    if (!this.handlers[message.type]) {
      throw new Error('No handler for message')
    }
    this.handlers[message.type].handle(message)
  }
}module.exports = Handlers
Finally, you may refactor your if-conditions into
something much more readable.
```

```
const Handlers = require("./engine/handlers");
const CreateNewGameHandler = require("./engine/
handler/create-new-game.handler");
const LeaveGameHandler = require("./engine/handler/
leave-game.handler");
const handlers = new Handlers({
  [CreateNewGameHandler.TYPE]: new
CreateNewGameHandler(games),
  [LeaveGameHandler.TYPE]: new LeaveGameHandler(games)
});
io.on("connection", socket => {
  socket.on("message", message => {
    handlers.handle({
      ...message,
      socketId: socket.id
    });
  });
  socket.on("disconnect", () => {
    handlers.handle({
      type: LeaveGame.TYPE,
      socketId: socket.id
    });
  });
});
```

However, there is one problem. How do you manage passing a message from a handler to the client? Should the handler be aware of any connected clients, or should it return something?

Internal Communication

Instead of making your handlers WebSockets-specific, consider how to keep them independent so that you may use them for other communication protocols.

The introduction of Events is a very beneficial decoupling strategy. When one of the handlers is ready to transmit something back to the client, it should send an internal messaging system a connection event. Any piece of code that cares about handling that event should keep an eye out for it. We might have customized code that listens for it, converts it to a message, and then sends it to a connected client.

EventEmitter or Subject from RxJS could be used to implement such communication. Only an instance of a publisher injected into your handlers is required.

```
const Handlers = require("./engine/handlers");
const CreateNewGameHandler = require("./engine/
handler/create-new-game.handler");
const LeaveGameHandler = require("./engine/handler/
leave-game.handler");
const handlers = new Handlers({
  [CreateNewGameHandler.TYPE]: new
CreateNewGameHandler(games),
  [LeaveGameHandler.TYPE]: new LeaveGameHandler
(games)
});
io.on("connection", socket => {
  socket.on("message", message => {
    handlers.handle({
      ...message,
      socketId: socket.id
    });
  });
  socket.on("disconnect", () => {
    handlers.handle({
      type: LeaveGame.TYPE,
      socketId: socket.id
    });
  });
});
```

Then, right from our handlers, you can publish as many events as you want.

```
class CreateNewGameHandler {
  constructor(games, eventBus) {
    this.games = games;
    this.eventBus = eventBus;
  }
handle(message) {
    const game = this.games.createNewGame(message.
payload.username);
    this.eventBus.next({
      type: "game-created",
```

```
      targets: game.players().map(player => player.id),
      payload: {
        gameId: game.id
      }
    });
  }
}
CreateNewGameHandler.TYPE = "create-new-game";
module.exports = CreateNewGameHandler;
```

A subscriber should listen to these events and convert them to WebSocket messages before providing them to clients.

```
const { Subject } = require("rxjs");
const eventBus = new Subject();
eventBus.subscribe(message => {
  message.targets.forEach(id => {
    io.to(id).emit("message", {
      type: message.type,
      payload: message.payload
    });
  });
});
```

HTTP versus WebSockets

Is this to say that creating a chat application without WebSockets is impossible?

HTTP Long Polling is a strategy that can help. The client submits a query, which the server holds open until new data is available. A fresh request is issued as soon as data appears and the client receives it, and the action is done over and over again. However, HTTP Long polling has a significant drawback in that it uses a lot of server resources.

Building a Chat Room App with Socket.io Tutorial

We will show one how to make a simple chat application with Vanilla JS frontend and Node.js server in the Socket.io tutorial below. Socket.io is a JavaScript module that enables bidirectional, real-time communication between connected clients (browsers) and the server.

CODE TUTORIAL

You must start by using the default package.json file to establish a project. Let us talk about the modules that were used in this project now.

- Express is a fast, unopinionated, simple web framework for node, according to expressjs.com.

- Nodemon is a utility that aids in the development of node.js-based apps by automatically restarting them when file changes in the directory are detected.

- **Babel** – Babel is a tool chain that converts ECMAScript 2015+ code into a backwards-compatible version of JavaScript in modern and legacy browsers and environments.

- Socket.IO offers bidirectional event-based communication in real time.

WHAT SOCKET.IO IS NOT?

Socket.IO is a WebSocket implementation, not a WebSocket implementation. Although Socket.IO uses WebSocket as a transport when possible, each packet contains additional metadata. As a result, a WebSocket client will be unable to connect to a Socket.IO server, and a Socket.IO client will be unable to connect to a plain WebSocket server.

After we have completed this, we will need to set up a server and install all of the required dependencies. We will need to build an index.js file and install socket.io and express to get started. The following command can be used: npm install express socket.io and npm install – save-dev nodemon and touch index.js, we will need to set up a local server and a simple socket connection in index.js. And, for the time being, that's all we have to do on the backend. The connection should be established once you submit a suitable request. It will be evident through the message that has been logged (as shown below).

```
const express = require("express");
const socket = require("socket.io");
// App setup
const PORT = 5000;
const app = express();
```

```
const server = app.listen(PORT, function () {
  console.log('Listening on port ${PORT}');
  console.log('http://localhost:${PORT}');
});
// Static files
app.use(express.static("public"));
// Socket setup
const io = socket(server);
io.on("connection", function (socket) {
  console.log("Made socket connection");
});
```

You Must Now Prepare the Frontend Portion

Let us begin by making the public folder and the files index.html and main.js. We can also include style.css. The index.html scaffold is shown below. All we need are some HTML tags to refer to and some Socket.io scripts included in the project. With the WebSockets scripts included, this is how the index.html file should look.

```
<!DOCTYPE html>
<html lang="en">
  <head>
    <meta charset="UTF-8" />
    <meta name="viewport" content="width=device-width,
initial-scale=1.0" />
    <title>Socket.io simple chat</title>
    <link rel="stylesheet" href="./style.CSS" />
  </head>
  <body>
    <div class="container">
      <div class="inbox">
        <div class="inbox__people">
          <h4>Active users</h4>
        </div>
        <div class="inbox__messages">
          <div class="messages__history"></div>
          <div class="fallback"></div>
        </div>
      </div>
```

```
      <form class="message_form">
        <input type="text" class="message_form__input"
placeholder="Type a message" />
        <button class="message_form__button"
type="submit">
          Enter
        </button>
      </form>
    </div>
    <script src="https://cdnjs.cloudflare.com/ajax/
libs/socket.io/2.3.0/socket.io.js"></script>
    <script src="main.js"></script>
  </body>
</html>
```

Then, on the frontend, you must set up the connection. In main, we simply need one line of code. const socket = io(); in js.

As we can see, the connection is established after the page is accessed and the script is loaded. The next step is to deal with a new user connection, a new message, and, last but not least, a user who is actively typing.

There are two ways to transmit data, such as events, in socket. One option is for the user to send an event to everyone (including the user), and the other is for the user to send an event to all other instances. The concept is to show a list of all active users. As a result, when a user connects, they must notify others and obtain a list of current users.

```
const activeUsers = new Set();
io.on("connection", function (socket) {
  console.log("Made socket connection");

  socket.on("new user", function (data) {
    socket.userId = data;
    activeUsers.add(data);
    io.emit("new user", [...activeUsers]);
  });
  socket.on("disconnect", () => {
    activeUsers.delete(socket.userId);
    io.emit("user disconnected", socket.userId);
  });
});
```

When a user connects, they send out an event that includes their username information. On the socket, you should set the userId property.
When the user disconnects, it will be required. Add a username to the set
of active users and emit an event with a list of all active users to accomplish this.

We have built two functions and two socket listeners in main.js.

```
const socket = io();
const inboxPeople = document.querySelector(".inbox__
people");
let userName = "";
const newUserConnected = (user) => {
  Username = user || 'User${Math.floor(Math.random()
* 1000000)}';
  socket.emit("new user", userName);
  addToUsersBox(userName);
};
const addToUsersBox = (userName) => {
  if (!!document.querySelector('.${userName}-
userlist')) {
    return;
  }
  const userBox = '
    <div class="chat_ib ${userName}-userlist">
      <h5>${userName}</h5>
    </div>
  ';
  inboxPeople.innerHTML += userBox;
};
// new user is created so we generate nickname and
emit event
newUserConnected();
socket.on("new user", function (data) {
  data.map((user) => addToUsersBox(user));
});
socket.on("user disconnected", function (userName) {
  document.querySelector('.${userName}-userlist').
remove();
});
```

To begin, we have generated a new user and emitted an event with that username (we can simply extend functionality by adding some prompt with a real user name). In addition, we have included them in the sidebar of all active users. On the server side, when a user disconnects, their username is removed from the set of current users and a disconnection event is emitted. Following that, they are deleted from the client's sidebar. Now that we've taken care of how users connect and disconnect, it's time to take care of the new messages.

On the server side, all you have to do is add the listener that is shown below.

```
socket.on("chat message", function (data) {
    io.emit("chat message", data);
});
```

We will need to do a few additional things on the client side, as seen in the example below.

```
const inputField = document.querySelector
(".message_form__input");
const messageForm = document.querySelector
(".message_form");
const messageBox = document.querySelector
(".messages__history");
const addNewMessage = ({ user, message }) => {
  const time = new Date();
  const formattedTime = time.toLocaleString("en-US",
{ hour: "numeric", minute: "numeric" });
const receivedMsg = '
  <div class="incoming__message">
    <div class="received__message">
      <p>${message}</p>
      <div class="message__info">
        <span class="message__author">${user}</span>
        <span class="time_date">${formattedTime}</span>
      </div>
    </div>
  </div>';
  const myMsg = '
  <div class="outgoing__message">
```

```
    <div class="sent__message">
      <p>${message}</p>
      <div class="message__info">
        <span class="time_date">${formattedTime}
</span>
      </div>
    </div>
  </div>';
  messageBox.innerHTML += user === userName?  myMsg :
receivedMsg;
};
messageForm.addEventListener("submit", (e) => {
  e.preventDefault();
  if (!inputField.value) {
    return;
  }
  socket.emit("chat message", {
    message: inputField.value,
    nick: userName,
  });
  inputField.value = "";
});
socket.on("chat message", function (data) {
  addNewMessage({ user: data.nick, message: data.
message });
});
```

The function that displays fresh messages is called immediately after receiving data from a socket. In the listener function of the form submit, the message is sent to the server. All we have to do now is see if the client is a message author. Now we will teach you how to send out the event that informs all other connections except your own. We would like to show that a user is currently typing something.

We must include socket.broadcast.emit on the server side. Take a peek at the list below (it is the final version of the file).

```
const express = require("express");
const socket = require("socket.io");
// App setup
const PORT = 5000;
const app = express();
```

```javascript
const server = app.listen(PORT, function () {
  console.log('Listening on port ${PORT}');
  console.log('http://localhost:${PORT}');
});
// Static files
app.use(express.static("public"));

// Socket setup
const io = socket(server);
const activeUsers = new Set();
io.on("connection", function (socket) {
  console.log("Made socket connection");
  socket.on("new user", function (data) {
    socket.userId = data;
    activeUsers.add(data);
    io.emit("new user", [...activeUsers]);
  });
 socket.on("disconnect", () => {
    activeUsers.delete(socket.userId);
    io.emit("user disconnected", socket.userId);
  });
socket.on("chat message", function (data) {
    io.emit("chat message", data);
  });
  socket.on("typing", function (data) {
    socket.broadcast.emit("typing", data);
  });
});
```

On the client side, the inputField keyup event listener and the socket listener on typing should be examined. Both of these things, as well as the final version of main.js, are seen below.

```javascript
const socket = io();

const inboxPeople = document.querySelector(".inbox__
people");
const inputField = document.querySelector(".message_
form__input");
const messageForm = document.querySelector(".message_
form");
```

```
const messageBox = document.querySelector
(".messages__history");
const fallback = document.querySelector(".fallback");

let userName = "";

const newUserConnected = (user) => {
  userName = user || 'User${Math.floor(Math.random()
* 1000000)}';
  socket.emit("new user", userName);
  addToUsersBox(userName);
};
const addToUsersBox = (userName) => {
  if (!!document.querySelector('.${userName}-
userlist')) {
    return;
  }
  const userBox = '
    <div class="chat_ib ${userName}-userlist">
      <h5>${userName}</h5>
    </div>
  ';
  inboxPeople.innerHTML += userBox;
};
const addNewMessage = ({ user, message }) => {
  const time = new Date();
  const formattedTime = time.toLocaleString("en-US",
{ hour: "numeric", minute: "numeric" });
  const receivedMsg = '
  <div class="incoming__message">
    <div class="received__message">
      <p>${message}</p>
      <div class="message__info">
        <span class="message__author">${user}</span>
        <span class="time_date">${formattedTime}
</span>
      </div>
    </div>
  </div>';
  const myMsg = '
  <div class="outgoing__message">
```

```
    <div class="sent__message">
      <p>${message}</p>
      <div class="message__info">
        <span class="time_date">${formattedTime}</span>
      </div>
    </div>
  </div>';
  messageBox.innerHTML += user === userName? myMsg :
receivedMsg;
};
// new user is created so we generate nickname and
emit event
newUserConnected();
messageForm.addEventListener("submit", (e) => {
  e.preventDefault();
  if (!inputField.value) {
    return;
  }

  socket.emit("chat message", {
    message: inputField.value,
    nick: userName,
  });
  inputField.value = "";
});
inputField.addEventListener("keyup", () => {
  socket.emit("typing", {
    isTyping: inputField.value.length > 0,
    nick: userName,
  });
});
socket.on("new user", function (data) {
  data.map((user) => addToUsersBox(user));
});
socket.on("user disconnected", function (userName) {
  document.querySelector('.${userName}-userlist')
.remove();
});
socket.on("chat message", function (data) {
  addNewMessage({ user: data.nick, message: data.
message });
});
```

```
socket.on("typing", function (data) {
  const { isTyping, nick } = data;
  if (!isTyping) {
    fallback.innerHTML = "";
    return;
  }
  fallback.innerHTML = '<p>${nick} is typing...</p>';
});
```

SUMMARY

As we can see, using Socket.io to create a chat app (or any other web app for that matter) with basic chat message features is not difficult. We hope that this brief Socket.io lesson demonstrated how simple it is to use this strategy. There are so many intriguing things you can do with JavaScript and a little understanding of Node.js. All of the code fragments, hints, and tricks described above should be quite self-explanatory. As we can see, making a few simple adjustments to the approach can make the WebSockets code more flexible and maintainable.

CHAPTER 3

Application Development II

IN THIS CHAPTER

➢ Streaming Apps

➢ Building apps with Node.js

➢ Keywords and Syntax

In the previous chapter, we learned about the development of a chat-based application using Socket.io. In this chapter, we will look into the development of one other application development that is based on video streaming. Before we jump into the code section, we must know a little about the streaming applications and its basic requirement.

When creating a streaming application, several factors must be considered, including functionality, the technological stack required, and cost analysis. Taking into account all factors and offering a better user experience for your clients necessitates careful planning, execution, product testing, monitoring, and performance maintenance, among other things. So here it is: a step-by-step guide on how to create a streaming app.

Disney debuted its over-the-top (OTT) services in 2019, and as of July 2021, the company had 116 million members. Disney Plus is also expected to reach more than 260 million paid members by 2024, according to

DOI: 10.1201/9781003357469-3

Variety. Disney's OTT platform has had success in areas other than movies and shows; for example, its ESPN+ service has around 1.71 million users.

We have already seen big streaming giants like Netflix, YouTube, Amazon Prime, HBO Max, and others that reap the rewards of enormous content demand. There's no disputing that developing a streaming app appeals to businesses, but there are various factors to consider.

STEP 1: PERFORM A MARKET STUDY

The first step in creating a streaming app is to identify the problem for which our app will provide a solution. As a result, market research is required to comprehend the current streaming app ecosystem, its consumers, and their problem concerns.

Streaming programming, for example, previously required a cable TV subscription. While this was the only option, it came with its own set of disadvantages, such as having to pay for channels we don't want to watch and incurring installation charges. The response was internet streaming software that allowed consumers to watch live TV channels without having to install anything and for a lower monthly fee. Similarly, depending on the problem you identify, there may be various use cases for streaming apps.

Here are a few examples of how streaming can be used.

There are two types of VOD platforms: cable-based VOD and OTT services. Another distinction is the medium; whereas cable-based VOD is based on TV streaming, OTT is based on video streaming over the internet.

OTT has three major subcategories:

- Subscription-based video-on-demand

- Transactional-based video on demand

- Advertisement-based video-on-demand

OTT and VOD applications have helped users with more choice-based streaming and access original content with monthly subscriptions, which was earlier limited to cinema halls.

Music Streaming Apps

Online music streaming apps have seen massive growth, being the leading contributor in the music industry apart from offline sales. While some music streaming applications offer a subscription-based service, others provide paid content.

eSports Streaming Apps

ESports streaming like Twitch has been quite popular. It's an eSports streaming service where you can stream gaming content uploaded by a massive community of gamers. Some of these apps also enable chat rooms and live scores for gaming events.

Understanding the pain points and building a streaming application based on the solution needs consideration of use cases with features that will serve such services. This is where we need to identify critical features and then design your application accordingly.

STEP 2: IDENTIFYING CHARACTERISTICS

For offering services and content access, streaming applications require specific features. If the app follows a freemium model, for example, where certain content is free but users must pay for other titles, a premium access function becomes necessary. As a result, based on the use cases, we will need to select a few critical elements for constructing a streaming platform.

Basic Characteristics

Login, profile management, admin panel, and other basic functions of a streaming application can be found. Although developing simple features may not appear to be difficult, we must consider factors such as user access, personalization, and user experience.

For example, if streaming service has a social login function, we will require social media API connections and security features like two-factor authentication. An authentication system can be used to add an extra layer of user verification by delivering a passcode or one-time password to their device.

Similarly, personalization capabilities that allow users to add numerous account profiles for profile management should be available. Users can also specify their location, allowing material to be tailored to the local streaming market. Understanding distinct service integrations, such as map service integration for a user location update, requires identifying such features. We can also add notifications and comments, where people can comment on their favorite movies, series, songs, and other content. Customers will receive notifications when new titles are added to your catalog or when a live eSports streaming event is taking place, depending on the use case.

Take YouTube, for example, where the entire app's model is based on user-generated content, making the video upload option indispensable. Along with the feature-supporting services like video format options, adding descriptions, video thumbnails, audio, and metals (titles and tags) are some important factors to think about.

Optional Extras

Depending on the use case, a streaming application will also require a number of sophisticated functionalities. An advanced search tool, for example, allows your customers to locate their favorite tiles and shows within the program. There are other features in addition to a sophisticated search option.

- There are numerous payment options available: Giving clients a variety of payment choices makes it simple for them to subscribe to your streaming services or purchase specific content online. We can even accept cryptocurrencies as a payment method, as the digital money is currently accepted in a number of nations.

- Multilanguage support is a must-have feature for streaming apps that cater to consumers from all over the world. Netflix, for example, provides audio in different languages for titles on its site.

- In-app chat: By enabling in-app chat, the users will be able to connect with other users on the platform and share their experiences with various types of content.

- Streamers can host or broadcast streams on their channels for other users to consume content. Streamers can broadcast live streams for other users on apps like Twitch and YouTube.

- Private streaming is a feature that allows broadcasters to broadcast their video privately to a single user, a group of users, or a specified region. Discord is one software that offers this type of private streaming option.

STEP 3: COMPLETION OF THE TECH STACK

There are various parts of each application's tech stack to consider. There are various distinct aspects of the tech stack to consider, ranging from development frameworks to deployment platforms. However, if we are seeking for a dependable video-streaming software, we will need to look no further then.

- Bitrate control or encoding for data transport
- Platforms for deploying
- Storage or databases
- Integrations to improve a variety of functions

Let us just explore at a few of the technicalities of a streaming app now.

Protocols for Online Video Streaming

Streaming is the process of delivering data to your device before it downloads or loads. This reduces the memory footprint and allows you to access data in a stream without interruption. The standard methods for executing such streams are known as streaming protocols.

MPEG-DASH

MPEG-DASH is a streaming protocol that stands for "Dynamic Adaptive Streaming over HTTP." It divides video content into small chunks and adjusts the quality for uninterrupted streaming based on the network's strength. A video stream will be divided into many parts of less seconds by the database or origin server. Furthermore, the server indexes these segments and encodes them for different devices to stream with different encoding standards.

HLS

HLS, or HTTP live streaming, is a streaming protocol similar to MPEG-DASH. It converts videos to downloadable HTTP files and sends them to the user's device using the HTTP protocol. These devices are capable of playing HTTP files in the same manner as they are capable of playing videos. As a result, because it works on any device with an internet connection, HLS is an excellent choice for the development of streaming applications.

RTMP

For live video streaming, RTMP (real-time messaging protocol) is employed. Most high-definition live streaming of concerts, for example, uses RTMP protocols. However, there are 10–20 s delays between the streaming source and the user's device. Using both the RTMP and HLS protocols together is one of the greatest ways for live streaming apps to reduce latency. The RTMP protocol provides for high-definition live streaming, whereas HLS uses adaptive bitrate streaming to reduce latency.

WebRTC

WebRTC is a real-time communication protocol that uses a streaming protocol. For data feed streaming, it works as a plugin and does not require a native application. WebRTC enables peer-to-peer communication by allowing audio/video feeds to be streamed in real time. WebRTC is used for video conferencing in Google Meet, Zoom, and other similar apps.

PLATFORMS FOR STREAMING

These are the platforms that will allow material to be streamed. Cloud-based solutions, for example, are an ideal choice for video-streaming applications that allow changing bitrates (VBR). To accommodate complex video parts, it modifies the data transport rate. As a result, it will fetch more data where there are complex segments, while the encoder will reduce the rate for optimization if there is less requirement for data transfer. We can develop a trigger function using cloud-based services by customizing a processing function. Bitrate control for improved video quality in streaming applications is possible with such triggers.

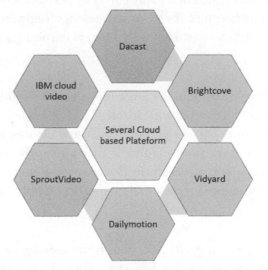

Several cloud-based platform for building a streaming app.

Correspondingly, we will need to choose the distribution infrastructure you want to use for our streaming app. If we really want to launch your app on the Google Play Store, for example, we will need a native streaming platform that is compatible with Android. Consider iOS, desktopOS, and other platforms as well.

CONTENT DISTRIBUTION NETWORKS

A streaming protocol such as HLS or MPEG-DASH splices the video into small chunks that are delivered to devices via a content distribution network (CDN). It refers to a globally distributed set of servers that enables for speedier internet content delivery. A CDN not only helps transport video content but also HTML pages, JavaScript files, stylesheets, photos, and audio files.

So, if we are trying to know and explore how to make a streaming app for the company, a CDN becomes one of the most important parts of your software stack. Users can benefit from configured CDNs because they can help with flawless streaming and safe data access.

The following are some of the benefits of selecting the correct CDN:

- CDNs use globally distributed servers to lessen the strain on a single server while also ensuring low latency.

- It allows for the collection of user statistics such as real-time load data, demand information on content assets, capacity per customer, trends, and consumption patterns, among other things.

- However, there are 20–30 s delays between the streaming source and the user's device.

- The availability of content for customers all over the world becomes a reality thanks to a distributed infrastructure, which aids in the scaling of your streaming business.

The best CDNs for streaming apps are:

- Amazon Cloudfront is a full-service cloud platform that enables streaming platforms, with support for HLS, DASH, HDS, and MSS broadcasts with 216 points of presence in 42 countries.

- Limelight Networks, with 130 points of presence in 70 countries, is one of the leading CDN service providers for streaming platforms.

- With around nearly 129 points of presence across 65 countries, Microsoft Azure offers a full-service cloud platform with storage that supports HLS, DASH, HDS, and MSS streams.

- Only the HLS protocol is supported by KeyCDN, which has 34 points of presence in 23 countries and ample documentation to get you started.

- With servers in 130 countries supporting HLS, HDS, and DASH protocols, Akamai is one of the major CDN services for streaming platforms.

- Provide HLS, MSS (Microsoft Smooth Streaming), HDS, and DASH streaming protocols through 60 points of presence in 30 countries.

Database and Hosting

We will need a dependable hosting service if you want to build a video-streaming platform. It enables one to deliver a seamless streaming experience for our audiences. Similarly, database requirements must be understood prior to the development of our streaming platform. We should think about cloud-based choices like Amazon S3 when thinking about our service's scalability. Such services might assist we are catering to a huge audience while also ensuring continuous streaming.

STEP 4: DEVELOPMENT AND DESIGN

It takes careful preparation to design our streaming application to include these capabilities and give a good user experience. Starting with the design stage, when a user interface (UI) wireframe is created for visualization. Then, with the client's agreement, an app development business can continue forward with developing a minimal viable product. Several things must be considered while designing a UI, including:

- Human-centric design: Placing the user at the center of the UI design process aids in the creation of simple-to-use programs.

- Organizational goals: The UI design must extend the organizational logic based on the use case and business requirements.

- UI designs that take into account a user's geographic location and ethnicity can have a significant impact on their user experience due to a sense of familiarity.

- Space heuristic: Taking advantage of various elements of the UI spaces can be beneficial; for example, you can introduce negative spaces for a more immersive experience.

- We may build the UI for the best experience by considering the accessibility of content for streaming applications.

STEP 5: TESTING AND UPKEEP

Streaming app testing is an important aspect of our development strategy since it ensures that our UI, backend server, API integrations, and other components operate well. Here, using automation technologies like Selenium and Appium will help us cut down on the time it takes to run various tests, allowing our company to fine-tune app performance.

There are several types of tests we will need to run for streaming applications, including:

- UX testing is used to guarantee that the user experience is consistent across all devices. Consistency, navigation, and functionality must all be tested across platforms.

- Load testing simulates peak demand on the system to check that your applications can handle increased loads. When millions of users consume content from your application from numerous places, load testing becomes critical.

- Performance testing examines the reliability, stability, and server performance in response to user content requests, regardless of bandwidth or platform. Such testing will allow us to ensure faultless streaming services and improved application performance.

- Checking linguistic clarity, cultural appropriateness of content, personalization, and accurate currency format for payment for local clients are all part of localization testing. It's a critical check to make sure that content localization matches user choices.

Maintaining optimal performance necessitates tracking many KPIs and fine-tuning the app's functionality. Maintenance, on the other hand, necessitates an understanding of the program's technology stack and architecture design in order to enable application functionality.

WHAT DOES IT COST TO CREATE A STREAMING APPLICATION?

Several factors must be considered when calculating the cost of producing a streaming application. It varies depending on the features' complexity, the developer involvement model, and a variety of other aspects. Understanding the costs aids in the formulation of a solid development strategy that yields optimal results.

Costs Dependent on Features

Functionality is extremely important when it comes to determining out how to develop a streaming app. If we are creating an SVOD OTT app, for example, we will need to provide a variety of features for consumers of various demographics. Multiple video resolution options, such as 4K or 1080P, as well as multilanguage audio adjustments, might take a long time to develop. Basic functions, such as user login and profile management, take less time to design because they are less complex. The question is, how can we determine the precise cost? Development time is the answer. It varies, however, depending on the type of application, its size, and characteristics. The cost of establishing a streaming application includes not just feature-based costs but also costs such as market research, ideation, testing, and maintenance.

APPLICATION DEVELOPMENT USING NODE.JS

If we are intending to create a streaming web application with numerous connections running at the same time, Node talents will undoubtedly be beneficial to us. When it comes to playing video in a web application, Node.js is the ideal choice because it divides data into pieces and plays large videos quickly.

Streams for Video Games

Data is sent to the client in segments rather than all at once, which is the case with Streams. In Node.js, there are streams that have a reputation for being difficult to work with and even more difficult to comprehend. Dominic Tarr argues, "Streams are Node's biggest and also most underappreciated concept." Even Dan Abramov, the creator of Redux and a member of the React.js core team, is terrified of Node streams.

What Exactly Are Streams?

Streams are one of the core principles that Node.js applications are built around. They are a data-handling method for sequentially reading or writing input into output. Streams are a technique to efficiently handle reading/writing files, network conversations, or any other type of end-to-end data flow. Streams are distinguished by the fact that, rather than reading a file into memory all at once as is the case with traditional methods, they read pieces of data piece by piece, processing its content without storing it entirely in memory. This makes streams extremely useful for dealing with enormous volumes of data. A file's size, for example, can exceed your allocated memory space, making it difficult to handle without reading the full file into memory. Streams come to the rescue in this situation. It is feasible to read larger files by using streams to handle smaller bits of data. Take, for example, "streaming" services like YouTube or Netflix: these services do not require you to download the video and audio feeds all at once. The browser instead receives the movie as a continuous stream of chunks, allowing receivers to begin watching and/or listening nearly immediately.

Streams, on the other hand, are not just for working with video or massive data. They also allow us the opportunity to write code that is "composable." When we design with composability in mind, we are ensuring that several components can be combined in a specific way to get the same outcome. Using streams in Node.js, you may create powerful chunks of code by piping data to and from smaller pieces of code.

Why use streams instead of other data-handling methods? Streams have two significant advantages over other data-handling methods:

- Memory efficiency means that we do not have to load vast amounts of data into memory before you can process it.

- Time efficiency: It takes far less time to begin processing data as soon as you receive it, rather than waiting until the complete payload has been transferred.

In Node, there are four different sorts of streams.js:

- Writable: Data can be written to streams. For example, fs.createWriteStream() allows us to use streams to write data to a file.

- Readable: Data streams that can be read. For example, fs.createReadStream() allows us to read a file's contents.

- Duplex streams are streams that can be read and written in both directions. Take, for example, the internet.

- Streams that can modify or transform data as it is written and read are known as socket transforms. In the case of file compression, for example, we can write compressed data to a file and receive decompressed data from it.

If we have worked with Node.js before, we have probably come across streams. In a Node.js-based HTTP server, for example, the request is a reading stream and the answer is a writable stream. It is possible that the fs module was used, which allows you to interact with both readable and writable file streams. Streams are used whenever you use Express to interface with the client because TCP sockets, TLS stack, and other connections are all built on Node.js streams. Streams are also used in every database connection driver that we can deal with.

A Real-Life Example

What is the most effective method for creating a readable stream?
We first create and initialize the Readable stream.

```
const Stream = require('stream')
const readableStream = new Stream.Readable()
```

We can transmit data to the stream now that it's been initialized:

```
readableStream.push('ping!')
readableStream.push('pong!')
```

Iterator in Asynchronous Fashion

When working with streams, using an async iterator is highly recommended. Asynchronous iteration, according to Dr. Axel Rauschmayer, is a mechanism for asynchronously retrieving the contents of a data container (meaning the current "task" may be interrupted before getting an item). It is also worth noting that the readable event is used inside the stream async iterator implementation. When reading from readable streams, we can use an async iterator:

```
import * as fs from 'fs';
async function logChunks(readable) {
  for await (const chunk of readable) {
    console.log(chunk);
  }
}
const readable = fs.createReadStream(
  'tmp/test.txt', {encoding: 'utf8'});
logChunks(readable);
// Output:
// 'This is a test!\n'
```

A string can likewise be used to capture the contents of a readable stream:

```
import {Readable} from 'stream';
async function readableToString2(readable) {
  let result = '';
  for await (const chunk of readable) {
    result += chunk;
  }
  return result;
}
const readable = Readable.from('Good noon !',
{encoding: 'utf8'});
assert.equal(await readableToString2(readable),
'Good morning!');
```

Because we intended to return a Promise, we had to utilize an async function in this scenario. It is crucial not to mix async methods with EventEmitter because there is presently no mechanism to detect a rejection when it is issued within an event handler, resulting in hard-to-trace issues and memory leaks. The current best practice is to encapsulate the content of an async function in a try/catch block and handle issues that way, although this is error prone. Once it gets on Node core, this pull request intends to fix the problem.

Creating Readable Streams from an Iterables Stream Using Readable. from()

Readable.from(iterable, [options]) is a convenience function for constructing Readable Streams from iterators that hold the data in iterable. There are two types of iterables: synchronous and asynchronous. The options parameter is optional and can be used to specify a text encoding, among other things.

```
const { Readable } = require('stream');
async function * generate() {
  yield 'hello';
  yield 'streams';
}
const readable = Readable.from(generate());
readable.on('data', (chunk) => {
  console.log(chunk);
});
```

Reading Modes

There are two reading modes available.

Reading streams, according to the Streams API, can be in one of two states: flowing or halted. Whether it's in flowing mode or halted mode, a Readable stream can be in object mode or not.

- In flowing mode, data is automatically read from the underlying system and given to an application using events via the EventEmitter interface as rapidly as feasible.

- The stream.read() method must be used directly to read chunks of data from the stream in paused mode.

To read data from a stream in flowing mode, we can listen to the data event and attach a callback. The readable stream broadcasts a data event when a chunk of data is available, and your callback executes. Take a look.

```
var fs = require("fs");
var data = '';
var readerStream = fs.createReadStream('file.txt'); //
Create a readable stream
readerStream.setEncoding('UTF8'); // Set the encoding
to be utf8.
// Handle stream events --> data, end, and error
```

```
readerStream.on('data', function(chunk) {
   data += chunk;
});
readerStream.on('end',function() {
   console.log(data);
});
readerStream.on('error', function(err) {
   console.log(err.stack);
});
console.log("Program Ended");
```

The fs.createReadStream() function creates a readable stream. The stream is initially in a static condition. It starts flowing as soon as we listen to a data event and attach a callback. Following that, data chunks are read and given to the callback. The frequency with which a data event is emitted is determined by the stream implementer. An HTTP request, for example, may produce a data event per few KBs of data read. We might elect to broadcast a data event once a line is read when reading data from a file. The stream produces an end event when there is no more data to read (end). We listen to this event in the excerpt above to be notified when it occurs. The stream produces an end event when there is no more data to read (end). We listen to this event in the snippet above to be notified when the end is reached.

In addition, if a mistake occurs, the stream will emit and warn the user.

All we have to do in paused mode is keep calling read () on the stream instance until all of the data is read, as seen in the following example:

```
var fs = require('fs');
var readableStream = fs.createReadStream('file.txt');
var data = '';
var chunk;
readableStream.on('readable', function() {
    while ((chunk=readableStream.read()) != null) {
        data += chunk;
    }
});
readableStream.on('end', function() {
    console.log(data)
});
```

The read() function returns data that has been read from the internal buffer. It returns null if there is nothing to read. As a result, we check for null in the while loop and end it. When a chunk of data from the stream can be read, the readable event is emitted. All Readable streams start out in paused mode, but they can be turned to flowing mode in one of several ways:

- Adding a handler for the "data" event.
- The method stream.resume() is being used.
- To send data to a writable, use the stream.pipe() method.

One of the following methods can be used to return the Readable to paused mode:

- By using the stream.pause() method if there are no pipe destinations.
- Remove all pipe destinations if there are any pipe destinations. The stream.unpipe() method can be used to delete multiple pipe destinations.

The key point to remember is that a Readable will not generate data unless it has a mechanism for either ingesting or ignoring it. The Readable will try to stop generating data if the consuming mechanism is disabled or removed. When we add a readable event handler, the stream will stop flowing and the data will be consumed using readable.read (). If the "readable" event handler is removed, the stream will resume flowing if a "data" event handler is present.

What Is the Most Effective Method for Creating a Writable Stream?

We must execute write () on the stream object to write data to a writable stream. As an example, consider the following:

```
var fs = require('fs');
var readableStream = fs.createReadStream('file1.txt');
var writableStream = fs.createWriteStream('file2.
txt');
readableStream.setEncoding('utf8');
readableStream.on('data', function(chunk) {
    writableStream.write(chunk);
});
```

The code shown above is simple. It simply reads data chunks from an input stream and publishes them to a destination using write (). If the procedure was successful, this function returns a Boolean value. If this is the case, the write was successful, and we can continue to write data. If false is returned, something went wrong and we are currently unable to post anything. By broadcasting a drain event, the writable stream will notify us when we can begin writing more data.

When we call the writable.end() method, we are telling the writable that no more data will be written to it. If a callback function is specified, it is attached as a listener for the "finish" event.

```
// Write 'hello, ' and then end with 'world!'.
const fs = require('fs');
const file = fs.createWriteStream('example.txt');
file.write('hello, ');
file.end('world!');
// Writing more now is not allowed!
```

A written stream can be used to read data from a readable stream:

```
const Stream = require('stream')
const readableStream = new Stream.Readable()
const writableStream = new Stream.Writable()
writableStream._write = (chunk, encoding, next) =>
{
    console.log(chunk.toString())
    next()
}
readableStream.pipe(writableStream)
readableStream.push('ping!')
readableStream.push('pong!')
writableStream.end()
```

We can also write to a writable stream using async iterators, which is encouraged.

```
import * as util from 'util';
import * as stream from 'stream';
import * as fs from 'fs';
import {once} from 'events';
```

```
const finished = util.promisify(stream.finished); //
(A)
async function writeIterableToFile(iterable, filePath)
{
  const writable = fs.createWriteStream(filePath,
{encoding: 'utf8'});
  for await (const chunk of iterable) {
    if (!writable.write(chunk)) { // (B)
      // Handle backpressure
      await once(writable, 'drain');
    }
  }
  writable.end(); // (C)
  // Wait until done. Throws if there are errors.
  await finished(writable);
}
await writeIterableToFile(
  ['One', ' line of text.\n'], 'tmp/log.txt');
assert.equal(
  fs.readFileSync('tmp/log.txt', {encoding: 'utf8'}),
  'One line of text.\n');
```

Pipeline ()

Piping is a method that allows us to feed the output of one stream into another. It's typically used to acquire data from one stream and pass that stream's output to another. The number of piping operations is unrestricted. To put it another way, piping is a technique for processing streaming data in several phases. Stream.pipeline was introduced in Node 10.x (). This is a module method for piping across streams, transmitting failures, cleaning up correctly, and providing a callback when the pipeline is finished.

Here's an example of how pipeline can be used:

```
const { pipeline } = require('stream');
const fs = require('fs');
const Zlib = require('zlib');
/ Use the pipeline API to simply connect a sequence of
streams
 and get informed when the pipeline is complete.
/ A pipeline for efficiently gzip-ing a potentially
large video file:
```

```
pipeline(
  fs.createReadStream('The.Matrix.780p.mkv'),
  zlib.createGzip(),
  fs.createWriteStream('The.Matrix.780p.mkv.gz'),
  (err) => {
    if (err) {
      console.error('Pipeline failed', err);
    } else {
      console.log('Pipeline succeeded');
    }
  }
);
```

Because pipe is dangerous, pipeline should be utilized instead.

The Stream Module

It is a part of software that allows us to create the stream module in Node. js serves as the foundation for all streaming APIs. The stream module is a native Node.js module that comes preinstalled. The stream object is an instance of the EventEmitter class, which in Node is used to handle asynchronous events. Streams are intrinsically event-based as a result of this.

To use the stream module, go to:

```
const stream = require('stream');
```

The stream module can be used to create new stream instances. To consume streams, we normally do not need to utilize the stream module.

Node APIs with Streams

Many Node.js core modules include native stream handling capabilities due to their benefits, the most notable of which are:

- net.Socket is the main node API on which streams are built, and it underpins the majority of the APIs that follow.

- The stdin command returns a stream that is connected to the stdin process.

- The stdout function returns a stream that is connected to the stdout process.

- The stderr function returns a stream that is attached to the stderr fs.

- createReadStream() produces a readable stream in the fs file.

- createWriteStream() establishes a file net with a writable stream.

- connect() establishes a stream connection.

- HTTP.request() returns a writable stream that is an instance of the HTTP.ClientRequest class.

- zlib.createGzip() compresses data into a stream using the gzip (compression algorithm).

- zlib.createGunzip() is a function that decompresses a gzip stream.

- zlib.createDeflate() compresses data into a stream using deflate (a compression method).

- zlib.createInflate() is a function that decompresses a deflate stream.

Here are some key dates in readable stream history:

- error – Emitted to signal that a writing/piping error has occurred.

- pipeline – This event is issued by the writable stream when a readable stream is piped into it.

- unpipe – Emitted when the reading stream is unpiped to prevent it from piping into the destination stream.

All of this was about the fundamentals of streams. The basic and most powerful elements of Node.js are streams, pipelines, and chaining. Streams can indeed assist you in writing clean and performant I/O code. There is also a Node.js strategic program called BOB that aims to improve Node.js streaming data interfaces, both internally and as future public APIs.

With this stream method, the client does not download the entire movie at once; instead, it downloads the first few seconds of the video and then waits for the preceding video to finish playing before downloading the next few seconds. When developing online apps, developers are constantly confronted with a variety of media, some of which can be difficult. We'll use Node.js to make our own video-streaming server in this article. If you follow this tutorial step by step, you'll be able to create a video-streaming server in Node.js that you can use in your own project.

OVERVIEW OF THE PROJECT

Let us have a look at how our app will work at a high level before we start coding. The browser is on the left, while the server is on the right in the image above. There will be an HTML5 video element on your site with a source that points to the/video endpoint.

The video element first sends a request to the server, after which the header delivers the necessary number of bytes from the video. For example, the requested range at the start of the video would be from the 0th byte onward, hence the 0-. The server will return a 206 HTTP status code, indicating that it is returning partial material with the appropriate header response, including the range and content length. The video element receives a message from the response headers indicating the video is unfinished. As a result, the video element will play the previously downloaded content. The video element will continue to make requests until no more bytes are available, at which point the cycle will repeat.

Advantages and Disadvantages of the Application

Let us look at some of the advantages and disadvantages of using this process now that we know how our app will work.

Our streaming server will be rather simple to create, as we could have predicted from the application summary. In essence, we're building a file system and handing it over to the client. Our server will let us choose times from the movie and determine how large a payload to send back. We went with 1 MB for mine, but we can do whatever we want with it.

However, due to the simplicity of our software, the server and video player do not operate as well as we would like. In essence, the video player will only request the portion of the film we are currently watching, disregarding what we have already requested. It is very possible that we will request some of the same resources multiple times.

CODE TUTORIAL

Starting at the beginning:

We'll start by creating a new folder and installing npm:

```
npm init
```

Install nodemon and Express now:

```
npm install —save express nodemon
```

Because your video element is an empty folder, we will need to create an HTML file that looks like this:

```
&lt;!DOCTYPE html>
<html lang="en">
    <head>
        <meta charset="UTF-8" />
        <meta HTTP-equiv="X-UA-Compatible"
content="IE=edge" />
        <meta name="viewport" content="width=device-
width, initial-scale=2.0" />
        <title>Video Streaming With Node</title>
        <style>
            body {
                margin: 10% auto;
                max-width: 90%;
                background-color: RGB(16, 16, 16);
                padding-top: 20%;
                padding-left: 55%;
            }
        </style>
    </head>
    <body>
        <video id="videoPlayer" width="100%" controls
muted="muted" autoplay>
            <source src="/video" type="video/mp3" />
        </video>
    </body>
</html>
```

The /Video Endpoint

After that, the/video endpoint will be written. When we will run the HTML code above, a media element should show on the screen eventually.

To make this work, we will need to make a new JavaScript file that contains all of our functions. We will need to create a new JavaScript file that contains all of our functions in order for this to work. In this new file, we will import Express and fs, which stands for file system. Run the following code:

```
const express = require("express");
const app = express();
const fs = require("fs");
app.get("/", function (req, res) {
    res.sendFile(__dirname + "/index.html");
});
// Just before the listening method, extra code will
be added.
app.listen(7000, function () {
    console.log("Listening on port 7000!");
});
```

We are going to make a function for the/video endpoint now. We must ensure that a range header is present. If we do not do so, we won't be able to tell the client which part of the video you wish to send back. The if statements take care of this, returning a 400 Error and informing the client that a range header is required:

```
app.get("/video", function (req, res) {
    const range = req.headers.range;
    if (!range) {
        res.status(400).send("Requires Range header");
    }
});
```

We'll also need to offer the video's route and size. There's no need to include a bunch of slashes if your movie is in the same directory as the JavaScript file. If the video isn't in the same directory as the JavaScript code, you'll need to specify the relative path, as seen below:

```
const videoPath = "Chris-Do.mp4";
const videoSize = fs.statSync("Chris-Do.mp4").size;
```

The following code block should now appear in the new file:

```
const express = require("express");
const app = express();
```

```
const fs = require("fs");
app.get("/", function (req, res) {
    res.sendFile(__dirname + "/index.html");
});
app.get("/video", function (req, res) {
    const range = req.headers.range;
    if (!range) {
        res.status(400).send("Requires Range header");
    }
    const videoPath = "Chris-Do.mp4";
    const videoSize = fs.statSync("Chris-Do.mp4").size;
});
app.listen(8000, function () {
    console.log("Listening on port 8000!");
});
```

Identifying the Range

The range will then be parsed; we are going to give it 1 MB at a time, which is called a chunk size:

```
const CHUNK_SIZE = 10 ** 6; // 1MB
const start = Number(range.replace(/\D/g, ""));
```

Now we'll parse the range headers for the first byte. Because it's a string, we have to convert it to a number with the following line:

```
const start = Number(range.replace(/\D/g, ""));
```

Because that is the last byte, we have deduct one from the video size in the end chunk. Because we start counting from zero in computer science, if a video has 100 bytes, the 99th byte is the last one.

We must now calculate the last byte that you will return. To begin, multiply the starting chunk by the chunk size, which is 1 MB. If the server keeps sending 1 MB back to the beginning chunk, the total size of the bytes sent could eventually exceed the size of the movie.

We have to return the video size in this scenario. We can accomplish so by using the Math.min function, which returns the lowest value of the two arguments given, as described by the line:

```
const end = Math.min (start + CHUNK_SIZE, videoSize - 1);
```

Creating Headers for Responses

We must now create the response headers that we will send back. To begin, multiply end-start + 1 by the content length. The headers object will then be created. We must utilize the initial byte, the ending byte, and the video size in the content range, as follows:

```
const headers = {
    "Content-Range": 'bytes
${start}-${end}/${videoSize}',
... / This simply indicates that there is additional
code in this area.
It is not a component of the code.
```

The video player uses the code above to determine how far along it is based on the video size. Following that, we'll specify the data type we'll send back. Add the video type and the length of the item. The code for your headers object should look like this:

```
const headers = {
    "Content-Range": 'bytes
${start}-${end}/${videoSize}',
    "Accept-Ranges": "bytes",
    "Content-Length": contentLength,
    "Content-Type": "video/mp4",
};
```

We must now compose a response to the request. We are the status code 206 to indicate that we are only sending a portion of the message. We need also make the following changes to the headers:

```
// HTTP Status 206 for Partial Content
res.writeHead(206, headers);
```

To generate the read stream, we'll use the file system library with the video path as an argument and the start and finish as options in the options object:

```
const videoStream = fs.createReadStream(videoPath,
{ start, end });
```

videoStream is completely self-contained. We must pipe it into the response we received at the beginning of the function:

```
videoStream.pipe(res);
```

If we have followed the instructions step by step, file should look like this:

```
const express = require("express");
const app = express();
const fs = require("fs");

app.get("/", function (req, res) {
    res.sendFile(__dirname + "/index.html");
});

app.get("/video", function (req, res) {
    const range = req.headers.range;
    if (!range) {
        res.status(400).send("Requires Range header");
    }
    const videoPath = "Chris-Do.mp4";
    const videoSize = fs.statSync("Chris-Do.mp4").
size;
    const CHUNK_SIZE = 16 ** 4;
    const start = Number(range.replace(/\D/g, ""));
    const end = Math.min(start + CHUNK_SIZE, videoSize
- 1);
    const contentLength = end - start + 1;
    const headers = {
        "Content-Range": 'bytes
${start}-${end}/${videoSize}',
        "Accept-Ranges": "bytes",
        "Content-Length": contentLength,
        "Content-Type": "video/mp4",
    };
    res.writeHead(206, headers);
    const videoStream = fs.createReadStream(videoPath,
{ start, end });
    videoStream.pipe(res);
});
```

```
app.listen(8000, function () {
    console.log("Listening on port 8000!");
});
```

Simply add "start": "nodemon index.js" to your package before wrapping up. JSON document:

```
"scripts": {
      "start": "nodemon index.js" //this is the main
line you need to add
},
//note that the index.js is just the name of my file.
yours might be named differently.
```

Simply run npm start to see the final result.

SUMMARY

We have learned how to use Node.js to create our own video-streaming server in this lesson. We went over the project architecture in detail first and then discussed the benefits and drawbacks of using a simple methodology. Then, by constructing the video endpoint, parsing the range, and creating the response headers, we can start building our app.

CHAPTER 4

Application Development III

IN THIS CHAPTER

➤ Concept of IoT

➤ Building Apps with Node.js

➤ Keywords and Syntax

IoT technology is still quite young, and it evolved in response to market demand for the ability to control a wide range of devices, sensors, and other equipment. Every device had its own interface, and a unified system that could handle large amounts of data was needed.

Today, more than half of businesses use the Internet of Things (IoT) to build new products. More and more developers are looking for the most efficient ways to design IoT platforms, utilizing the finest programming languages and tools available. Because it is such a new field, there is no one-size-fits-all answer, yet many businesses are seeking for the best ways to develop IoT initiatives.

WHY IS NODE.JS THE BEST IOT SOLUTION?

In today's world, smart devices are becoming more and more common. Smartwatches, microwave ovens, washing machines, and even homes are all examples of this. All of them are in perfect sync with your smartphone.

DOI: 10.1201/9781003357469-4

We simply download an app that allows you to manage dozens of procedures carried out by your smart devices. This is where the IoT's magic starts. It allows us to sync our mobile app with all of our home's smart technologies in real time.

We use a variety of computer languages to construct such solutions, including Python, Java, C++, and Ruby. They can all take care of establishing IoT systems and do it well. However, when it comes to programming languages created particularly for this purpose, they all pale in comparison to JavaScript, which is the best for working with IoT. JavaScript isn't ideal in and of itself, but that's where Node.js comes in. Node.js offers a large community, a large number of libraries, and the ability to function reliably on large projects without consuming a lot of server resources. Node.js is a server-side environment that executes code. It is used by developers to create large, versatile projects. It is a really powerful tool that is also quite simple to understand. Even a developer who isn't very familiar with JavaScript will be able to use it.

First and foremost, we would like to dispel some Node.js fallacies propagated by folks who haven't looked at the repository's Changelog Git and have no idea how the technology has progressed.

WHAT EXACTLY ARE THE ADVANTAGES OF NODE.JS FOR IOT?

To begin, Node.js is an open-source, cross-platform runtime environment that is used by businesses of all sizes to create fast, scalable applications. It is a powerful tool that programmers eagerly employ for a variety of projects.

Application Development Using Node.js

Node.js also has a large developer community, several IoT libraries, and the ability to work on projects steadily without consuming a lot of server resources. Here are several reasons to choose Node.js for IoT platform and app development.

IoT Protocols Are Simple to Integrate with Node.js

Integration is one of the most important aspects of the IoT. The MQTT protocol, which is widely used by IoT apps, is supported by Node.js, enabling it simply to access to third-party services and preparing it for inclusion in a variety of scenarios. Back-end integration is carried out.

MQTT.js is used by all Node.js IoT SDKs from leading cloud providers. An example of such integration is AWS IoT Node.js. Using MQTT, it can analyze and route millions of messages reliably to AWS endpoints and other devices.

Node.js Is a Powerful and Quick Programming Language

Any IoT device, as previously said, operates with rapidly changing data. As a result, it will require a powerful IoT platform capable of handling enormous data volumes in real time.

Node.js includes node-packaged modules (NPM), which provide sophisticated repositories for IoT needs. Node.js transforms JavaScript into native machine code for fast execution, thanks to Google's V8 engines. Over 80 Arduino controller packs, as well as various packages for Pebble and Fitbit wearables, are available in the NPM repository. Built-in IoT architectures for Bluetooth devices and sensors are also proposed.

Node-RED, a flow-based programming tool, allows you to create low-code IoT applications. In the IoT world, the ability to develop C++ modules is extremely useful. C drivers exist for much of the hardware, allowing developers to connect it into Node.

Node.js Is a Scalable and Resource-Efficient Programming Language

Because Node.js takes less time to execute, it consumes fewer resources than an app written in Java or Ruby, for example. A standard 8 GB RAM device, for example, can support 4,000 concurrent connections at once, with each thread consuming 2 MB of memory. This identical device can support one million simultaneous connections using Node.js.

Data Security Is Provided by Node.js

We connect several devices to a single network in the IoT to exchange data for a unique task. Interactivity and device connections are required for proper execution. Security includes three components for IoT devices:

- Authenticating devices and users; access privileges to various functionalities.

- Code architecture that is constantly evolving.

- These requirements can be met with Node.js.

Authentication That Is Safe

Tokens, auth0, jwt, and other authentication mechanisms are available for Node.js apps. Each has its own set of merits and demerits when viewed through the lens of the IoT. Tokens are useful, but they aren't totally secure. They're a terrific technique to authenticate because they let you identify a specific user and decide whether or not to provide them access.

Even an encrypted token or login/password data is stored in firmware by the IoT ecosystem. Someone can steal the token if they have physical access to the device, which also applies to jwt and auth0.

By integrating any server-side authentication tools into the Node.js framework, we can use them and may accomplish this manually with Node Package Manager: passport, auth0, and jwt. Packages for integrating cloud services, such as Azure IoT hub Node.js or AWS-IoT, are also available. Even an encrypted token or login/password data is stored in firmware by the IoT ecosystem. Someone can steal the token if they have physical access to the device, which also applies to jwt and auth0. By integrating any server-side authentication tools into the Node.js framework, you can use them. We may accomplish this manually with Node Package Manager: passport, auth0, and jwt. Packages for integrating cloud services, such as Azure IoT hub Node.js or AWS-IoT, are also available.

It's Easy to Create APIs with Node.js

The ability to construct APIs is another advantage of Node.js. LinkedIn developers, for example, were the first to use Node.js development tools to create a mobile API. Node.js frameworks are used to construct web services and APIs on the platform. Because it simply takes a few lines of code to develop an API with Node.js, it can be done rapidly.

Where Can I Begin Developing an IoT Project in Node.js?

When we first start working on an IoT project, the first thing that comes to mind is: where do you begin? Do you design your own architecture or select all of the modules we will need? Perhaps you should start with a database?

It's a lot easier than it appears. The first step is to design a database architecture that includes all fields. We will need it to get the most out of your project. Because of the bad system architecture, we could get delayed requests or even get stuck in the middle of development if we don't have it. Databases are the most susceptible part of IoT projects, and they're also the most difficult to modify. The architecture should be as adaptable as feasible, and it should be suited for the integration of new technologies.

The best solution is to employ the Hierarchical Model—View—Controller pattern, in which each system component has a role in the larger scheme and follows the MVC design.

After we have decided on database architecture, consider how the data will be updated, at what frequency, and in what quantity. Almost all IoT services have a ready-to-use solution for your issue. After we have decided on database architecture, consider how the data will be updated, at what frequency, and in what quantity. Almost all IoT services have a ready-to-use solution for your issue. AWS IoT, for example, includes a "Rules" capability that allows a developer or DevOps to arrange data. We can select where our data is stored, which database to use, which script to run for additional data processing, and so on. We should be highly familiar with the service's functioning so that we don't end up having to reinvent the wheel. Services like ASW are designed to make your life easier, and if we don't utilize them, we are missing out.

How Do You Pick the Best Database for IoT?

Modern databases can link to IoT databases; however, it all depends on how a developer implements the connection. Before we choose a database, we must determine whether it is appropriate for the capabilities we will deliver to your users. The following is a list of the database's primary functions:

- Indexes are supported and the design is flexible.

- User-friendly scheme that can withstand high volumes of data.

- Data export and import are supported.

- Various parameters are used to perform a multifunctional search.

- Security.

- A good price-to-quality ratio.

When it comes to launching an IoT project, it is up to each individual to decide which features should be prioritized. However, using a number of different databases for our projects isn't a bad idea. It's possible that a project's design is so sophisticated that only one database will be able to meet all of the functional requirements. Important to remember: for a simple operation, you don't need a powerful database; instead, utilize a highly specialized one.

- InfluxDB: Since 2013, InfluxDB has been the best database for IoT programming. It's an open-source time-series database created in the Go programming language. It is excellently designed for IoT, which has contributed to its continued popularity.

- CradeDB is a SQL database that is distributed as open-source code developed in Java. Its main advantage is the list of libraries it offers, such as Facebook Presto, Apache Lucene, and ElasticSearch, which don't require any additional configuration and make your life a lot easier. This database is ideal for integrating into a variety of IoT platforms.

- MongoDB is a NoSQL database that is free to use. It is every developer's best friend who has written at least one Node.js project's best friend. It's simple to use and features a JSON-like architecture that works nicely with JavaScript. MongoDB may not be the ideal answer for building an IoT platform, but it is for integrating Node.js into the platform.

- Amazon DynamoDB is a closed-source time series database that is one of Amazon's online services. It is best to utilize with other services offered by the company, as with other analogs (Cloud Bigtable or IBM Informix). In this situation, AWS IoT with DynamoDB provides a powerful framework for building heavily loaded IoT projects. It's a bad idea to utilize this database on its own, but there are plenty of different analogs that can achieve the same purpose.

After comparing several modern IoT databases, what conclusions can we draw? We all are suited for IoT platform development, but each has its own set of capabilities. So, depending on your requirements, make an informed decision.

How to Make Big Data Work for IoT Projects

So, in our IoT project, we chose the primary technological stack, thought through the architecture of both databases and servers, and now it's time to start developing. The initial step is to determine which section of the project will be the most heavily loaded and how to optimize it. If we utilize a complicated solution (e.g., AWS IoT with DynamoDB), AWS will bear the brunt of the demand, ensuring that all of our data is processed appropriately, regardless of volume. On the contrast, there are a few solutions that can assist us if we build the architecture on our own server. Let us mind few things in mind to make our optimization process go more smoothly.

The Project's Future Architecture Will Be Able to Grow with It

Most developers use Docker containers and a load balancer to automatically scale their projects. Regardless of whether we use AWS ECS or HAProxy, we must understand how this technology works, how to configure it, and how to maintain it. Many development issues arise as a result of the developer's lack of understanding on how to configure the system that has been recommended by the community. Everyone selects the one that best meets their requirements.

The Work with the Project's Code Is the Next Step in Optimization

We must understand how Node.js works, as well as its advantages and disadvantages. The ideal method to work with Big Data is to design an architecture that only handles a tiny portion of the project. The projects must keep track of their progress and have the option to test their functionality in isolated sandboxes. We should be aware that Node.js in IoT provides the developer with a variety of options for solving the problem; therefore, it's ideal to follow the best practices for working with heavily loaded systems:

- Heavy activities must be processed by code through a queue.

- Data cashing is required for your project.

- The database requests should be as efficient as feasible.

- You can be sure that your IoT platform will be quick and stable no matter how much data it processes if you keep your architecture basic and follow these best practices.

Real-Time IoT Analytics

In most cases, the IoT platform's primary function is to collect data from hundreds or even thousands of sensors and provide it to consumers.

Everything in the modern world has to work in real time and has a clean and clear interface to display data. For those who must strike a balance between working quickly and keeping things simple in production, analytics development is a significant challenge. Many people believe that it is best to use a premade solution and customize it to our project's requirements. If our project does not require extremely particular features, this is the best approach. Someone, somewhere, may have already dealt with your issues and devised a solution. So why not put it to good use? However, because no two IoT projects are alike, you must carefully consider the details of your product.

If we need to construct real-time analytics but don't have a lot of time, AWS is a good place to start. We can also trust on the internet to locate solutions based on open-source code that we can easily integrate into the system and use.

Sure, we can link the web client to the IoT and output data directly, but security concerns may arise. It's crucial to know what we are giving users, how they should authorize themselves, and whether the system can manage the users and their access levels. The ideal solution is to divide the IoT into different WebSockets on the server, which will filter the data and have no direct impact on the IoT. We should also bear in mind that memory leaks must be avoided when developing data transmission over WebSocket. Also, when it comes to data preparation and transfer to analytics, try not to overcomplicate things.

The browser's capability is used to determine all JavaScript actions. The browser may slow down or possibly crash if the data flow is too large. For experienced coders, this isn't a problem because they're used to dealing with delays, currency, and data filtration. Always consider the audience for whom our project is intended and tailor everything to their requirements. The majority of developers use popular frameworks or libraries to create single-page application web applications (angular or react).

What Are Some Examples of Node.js-Based IoT Apps?

The Node.js ecosystem's maturity is critical for the IoT. But when should you utilize Node.js? Here are some instances from actual life:

Uber

Uber's primary trip execution engine is based on Node.js. The key reasons for this decision were asynchrony, the ability to analyze large amounts of data, clean code, and a low cost of implementation.

Code Tutorial

There are now a slew of firms devoted to Uber-for-X apps. The theory is that if Uber can do it for cabs, they can certainly do it for other supply/demand issues. So we decided to make a citizen-cop app during a hackathon. We thought it would be fun to create something that can assist your pals in times of need!

Following are the features that we agreed on after some thought:

- At the touch of a button, residents will be able to request the nearest police officer in their area. It will send out a "distress signal," alerting nearby cops.

- Any police officers in the area will be alerted to the user's location and will have the option of accepting the request and resolving the problem.

- A grading scale.

- Data gathered from locations, solved crime cases, and so on can be shown on a map or graphed using some creative user interface widgets.

Every app you create now has a few key components:

- On the back end, there's a client-facing app (that you see in a browser or on your phone screen).

- Incoming client requests and information are routed through a web server.

- Information.

- Is stored in a database that may be queried.

MongoDB will be your database on the back end. It's simpler to understand and provides a wide range of querying techniques for geospatial data, which we will need for our project.

For our back-end logic, we will utilize NodeJS. Because the frontend and backend are written in the same language, we won't have to worry about learning a new language or grammar.

You'll use HTML5, CSS3, JavaScript, and the Google Maps and Places APIs on the front end.

We are presuming that user are already aware about JavaScript and have a basic understanding of how NodeJS and MongoDB function.

Let's get this party started!

For a long time, developers have relied on MongoDB to create applications. It has a short learning curve, and its adaptability enables developers to create applications quickly and easily.

MongoDB is one of my favorite databases since it helps me to quickly prototype ideas and present proof-of-concept.

Make sure you have MongoDB and NodeJS installed before you begin. The latest version of MongoDB is 5.0 at the time of writing this chapter.

The Schema's Design

Everything you save in MongoDB is a collection of documents since we are utilizing it.

Let's make a citizensData collection for collecting citizen information and a policeData collection for storing officer information. So, open a terminal window and type mongo to launch the mongo shell. Once it's open, type: to see a list of existing MongoDB databases.

```
display DBS
```

To store our app's data, you'll need a new database. Let's refer to it as myUberApp. We can create a database by typing:

```
Use myUberApp
```

The use command generates a new database if one does not already exist. If it does, Mongo is instructed to run the following procedures on this database. Mongo organizes its data into collections. Tables are similar to collections. To view what collections are already available, type:

```
displaying collections
```

The badge-id could also be the username for the cop. For authentication purposes, you might provide a field for e-mail address and a field for password (which will not be exposed). Save the JSON dataset for cop-related information.

```
{
    "userId" : "01",
    "displayName" : "Cop 1",
    "phone" : "01",
    "email" : "cop01@gmail.com",
    "earnedRatings" : 21,
    "totalRatings" : 25,
    "location" : {
        "type" : "Point",
        "address" : "SS Environs, Chellikere, 1st
block, Chelekare, Kalyan Nagar, Bengaluru, Karnataka
560043, India",
        "coordinates" : [
            77.63997110000003,
            13.0280047
        ]
    }
}
{
    "userId" : "02",
    "displayName" : "Cop 2",
    "phone" : "02",
    "email" : "cop02@gmail.com",
    "earnedRatings" : 10,
    "totalRatings" : 25,
    "location" : {
        "type" : "Point",
        "address" : "Artistic Art Forum Pvt.ltd, HAL
2nd Stage, Appareddipalya, Indiranagar, Bengaluru,
Karnataka 560038, India",
        "coordinates" : [
            77.64115449999997,
            12.9718915
        ]
    }

}
```

```
{
    "userId" : "03",
    "displayName" : "Cop 3",
    "phone" : "03",
    "email" : "cop03@gmail.com",
    "earnedRatings" : 15,
    "totalRatings" : 25,
    "location" : {
        "type" : "Point",
        "address" : "16, D Bhaskaran Rd, Murphy Town,
Ulsoor, Bengaluru, Karnataka 560008, India",
        "coordinates" : [
            77.62855850000005,
            12.9817147
        ]
    }
}
{
    "userId" : "04",
    "displayName" : "Cop 4",
    "phone" : "04",
    "email" : "cop04@gmail.com",
    "earnedRatings" : 11,
    "totalRatings" : 25,
    "location" : {
        "type" : "Point",
        "address" : "77-406, MG Road, Shanthala Nagar,
Shivaji Nagar, Bengaluru, Karnataka 560001, India",
        "coordinates" : [
            77.60547099999997,
            12.975614
        ]
    }
}
{
    "userId" : "05",
    "displayName" : "Cop 5",
    "phone" : "05",
    "email" : "cop05@gmail.com",
    "earnedRatings" : 15,
    "totalRatings" : 25,
    "location" : {
```

```
        "type" : "Point",
        "address" : "Swamy Vivekananda Rd,
Gowthamapuram, Jogupalya, Bengaluru, Karnataka 560007,
India",
        "coordinates" : [
            77.62047400000006,
            12.972814
        ]
    }
}
{
    "userId" : "06",
    "displayName" : "Cop 6",
    "phone" : "06",
    "email" : "cop06@gmail.com",
    "earnedRatings" : 21,
    "totalRatings" : 25,
    "location" : {
        "type" : "Point",
        "address" : "869, 12th Main Rd, Koramangala 3
Block, Koramangala, Bengaluru, Karnataka 560034,
India",
        "coordinates" : [
            77.62710779999998,
            12.9279232
        ]
    }
}
{
    "userId" : "07",
    "displayName" : "Cop 7",
    "phone" : "07",
    "email" : "cop07@gmail.com",
    "earnedRatings" : 18,
    "totalRatings" : 25,
    "location" : {
        "type" : "Point",
        "address" : "7th Cross Rd, Domlur I Stage,
Stage 2, Domlur, Bengaluru, Karnataka 560071, India",
        "coordinates" : [
            77.63873160000003,
```

```
            12.9609857
        ]
    }
}
```

In our terminal, type the following to import data from this JSON file:

```
mongoimport --DB myUberApp --collection policeData
--drop --file ./path/to/jsonfile.json
```

Now, before beginning querying your database, we should familiarize ourselves with how indexes in MongoDB (or any database) function. An index is a data structure or a particular arrangement of data that allows you to search for information quickly. This allows you to access results quickly without having to search the full database.

For example, suppose you kept student information in a book in ascending order of their names, implying that we have an index on the name field. That way, if we needed information on a person named Tyrion, we could instantly find it without having to look through the rest of the pupils.

However, if the same information was recorded in ascending order of their height, finding information for a person by name would be difficult. Because the students are no longer saved in order of their names, we may have to scan and search over numerous rows, which could take a long time. However, different types of inquiries are now possible. Get information on kids who are between the heights of 4 and 5 feet, for example. In which situation, Tyrion's information might be immediately acquired because different types of indexes are supported by different databases. The complete list of indexes that support MongoDB can be found here.

So, if you type the following command:

```
DB.policeData.find().pretty()
```

returns all documents contained within the policeData collection, which is the whole list of officers. We can use the command db.policeData.find(userId: "01") to get information on a specific cop whose userId is

```
1. pretty()
{
    "_id" : ObjectId("57e75af5eb1b8edc94406943"),
    "userId" : "01",
    "displayName" : "Cop 1",
    "phone" : "01",
    "email" : "cop01@gmail.com",
    "earnedRatings" : 21,
    "totalRatings" : 25,
    "location" : {
        "type" : "Point",
        "address" : "Kalyan Nagar, Bengaluru,
Karnataka 560043, India",
        "coordinates" : [
            77.63997110000003,
            13.0280047
        ]
    }
}
```

Geospatial Indexes in MongoDB

GeoJSON objects can be stored in documents using geospatial indexes. GeoJSON objects come in a variety of shapes and sizes, including Point, LineString, and Polygon. If you look at the result of your.find() command, we will note that each location is an object with a type field and coordinates field. This is significant because the $near command can be used to query for points within a specific distance for a particular longitude and latitude of your GeoJSON object is of the Point type.

We will need to construct a 2D sphere index (a geographic index) on the location field and a type field within it to use this. The 2D sphere index can be used to calculate geometries on a sphere that resembles the earth. This comprises geographical searches in MongoDB, such as those for inclusion, intersection, and proximity.

So, in your mongo shell, type:

```
createIndex("location": "2dsphere"), db.policeData.
createIndex("location": "2dsphere"), db.policeData.
createIndex("location": "2d
```

To get documents from the closest to the farthest away from a given pair of coordinates, use the following syntax:

```
DB.<collectionName>.find({

    <fieldName>: {

        $near: {

            $geometry: {

                type: "Point",

                coordinates: [<longitude>, <latitude>]

            },

            $minDistance: <distance in metres>,

            $maxDistance: <distance in metres>
        }
    }
}).pretty()
createIndex("location": "2dsphere"), db.policeData.
createIndex("location": "2dsphere"), db.policeData.
createIndex("location": "2d
```

To get documents from the closest to the farthest away from a given pair of coordinates, use the following syntax:

$minDistance and $maxDistance are two variables that can be used to calculate distance. Fields like distance are optional. Now, run this command to find all cops within 2 kilometers of latitude 12.9718915 and longitude 77.64115449999997.

```
DB.policeData.find({
    location: {
        $near: {
            $geometry: {
                type: "Point",
                coordinates: [77.64115449999997,
12.9718915]
            },
```

```
            $maxDistance: 2000
        }
    }
}).pretty()
```

That's all there is to it: The output will contain a list of documents. Perfect! Let's apply the same logic to a web server. This package.json file should be downloaded and saved in the root of our project folder (name it package.json), then cd to the directory containing the file and execute it from our terminal.

```
npm install sudo
```

Here's a quick rundown of some of the packages we will be using:

- Express is a NodeJS web framework. It contains a large ecosystem of APIs, tools, and middleware to assist you in developing your application.

- Before your handlers, body-parser parses incoming request bodies in a middleware, which is accessible via the req.body parameter. This is required in order to handle POST requests.

- The underscore character makes it easier to write JavaScript. If you prefer, you are free to utilize another library.

- You can use web sockets in your Node application with socket.io.

- The official MongoDB NodeJS driver is MongoDB. It allows your Node program to communicate with your database.

Other modules are also included in the package.json file. We will need them while creating a complete app, but we will focus on how to use the MongoDB driver to perform queries in our express app. The following are the functions of some of the other modules:

- In NodeJS, async is a utility for dealing with asynchronous programming. It aids in the avoidance of callback hell.

- debug is a library for debugging. This useful application allows you to debug your programs without having to utilize the ugly console. outputs of the log statement.

- The MongoDB driver is comparable to redis. It allows your NodeJS application to communicate with your Redis database.

- connect-redis is a session store that manages sessions with Redis. When you decide to have user accounts, you'll need this information.

It's a good idea to organize your code before you start writing it. You can use the following two files for the time being:

A file where you can write your API endpoints. A database-related file that makes use of database drivers. The route handler would determine which database function to call. Following the execution of a query, the results are returned to your route handler via a callback function.

Let's have a look at what this looks like in code:

```
var HTTP = require("HTTP");
var express = require("express");
var consolidate = require("consolidate"); //1
var _ = require("underscore");
var bodyParser = require('body-parser);

var routes = require('./routes'); // File has our
endpoints
var mongoClient = require("mongodb").MongoClient;

var app = express();
app.use(bodyParser.urlencoded({
   extended: true,
}));

app.use(bodyParser.json({limit: '10mb'}));

app.set('views', 'views'); //Set the folder-name from
where you serve the html page.
app.use(express.static('./public')); //setting the
folder name (public) where all the static files like
css, js, images etc. are made available

app.set('view engine','html');
app.engine('html',consolidate.underscore);
var portNumber = 7000; //for locahost:7000
```

```
http.createServer(app).listen(portNumber, function(){
//creating the server which is listening to the port
number:7000, and calls a function within in which
calls the initialize(app) function in the router
module
  console.log('Server listening at port '+
portNumber);
  var url = 'mongodb://localhost:27417/myUberApp';
  mongoClient.connect(url, function(err, db) { //a
connection with the mongodb is established here.
    console.log("Connected to Database");
    routes.initialize(app, db); //function defined in
routes.js which is exported to be accessed by other
modules
  });
});
```

/* 1. (consolidate) is a command that makes the template engines work in a consistent manner. It does not have any modules of its own, and any template engine that is to be utilized must be installed separately.!*/

We will construct a new instance of the MongoClient object from the MongoDB module in this example. We can connect to our MongoDB database using the connect function exposed by your MongoClient instance once the web server has started. The function returns a Db instance in the callback after it has initialized the connection. We can now send both the app and DB instances to your routes.js file's initialize function.

Then, in a new file called routes.js, paste the following code:

```
function initialize(app, DB) {
    //A GET request to /officers must return a list of
local cops.
    app.get('/cops', function(req, res){
    /* retrieve the latitude and longitude info from
the request. Then, fetch the nearest cops using
MongoDB's geospatial queries and return it back to the
client.
    */
    });
}
exports.initialize = initialize;
```

We will need to pass the coordinates as query strings in your request for this to work. In a separate file, we will write your database operations. So, make a new file called DB-operations.js and write the following:

```
function fetchNearestCops(DB, coordinates, callback) {
    DB.collection('policeData').createIndex({
        "location": "2dsphere"
    }, function() {
        DB.collection("policeData").find({
            location: {
                $near: {
                    $geometry: {
                        type: "Point",
                        coordinates: coordinates
                    },
                    $maxDistance: 2000
                }
            }
        }).toArray(function(err, results) {
            if(err) {
                console.log(err)
            }else {
                callback(results);
            }
        });
    });
}
exports.fetchNearestCops = fetchNearestCops;
```

This function takes three arguments: a DB instance, an array of coordinates in the order [longitude>,latitude>], and a callback function to which the results of your query are returned.

If we have previously generated an index on the selected field, you might wish to skip the create Index step if we have already done so before querying.

Now all we need to do is call this function from within your handler. As a result, alter our routes. This is the js code for it:

```
var dbOperations = require('./db-operations');
function initialize(app, DB) {
```

```
// '/cops?lat=12.9718915&&lng=77.64115449999997'
app.get('/cops', function(req, res){
    //Convert the query strings into Numbers
    var latitude = Number(req.query.lat);
    var longitude = Number(req.query.LNG);
    dbOperations.fetchNearestCops(DB,
[longitude,latitude], function(results){
    //JSON should be returned to the client as a
result
        res.json({
            cops: results
        });
    });
});
}
exports.initialize = initialize;
That's all there is to it! Run
app.js in node.js
login to the browser and go to http://localhost:8000/
cops?lat=12.9718915&lng=77.64115449999997 from your
terminal.
```

We should receive a JSON response containing either an empty array or an array containing cop data, depending on the query strings you gave. In the meantime, check out the GitHub repository for the source code!

SUMMARY

In this chapter, we have tried to cover a wide range of topics related to IoT project development that can be used to heavily loaded systems. First and foremost, developers must recognize the functionality that an IoT platform requires and implement it using the tools available to them. The programming world does not stand still, and new solutions to various issues arise every day. We must always be aware of all new things that appear, or else we will be left behind. The IoT platform trains we need to be disciplined and does not easily tolerate mistakes. Losing data or incorrectly processing it could have disastrous effects for the firm and all users who relied on the solution. The development team must always approach the project in the best possible way, anticipating all of the issues that the platform may encounter. First and foremost, identify the architecture, as well as the external solutions to be used and how they will be managed. We will never know for sure if your solution is totally functional, but it's better to be safe than sorry by testing it on a real-world project. Of course, this isn't always the case; in some circumstances, developers must deviate from the guidelines, but they must justify the goal they've established. Never get too attached to a single technology or service and constantly be willing to try new things. Perhaps a new library or framework can solve all of the issues you've been having with older technology. Decide how we will test this out, because Big Data is difficult to build and monitor in any case. We will be all correct if we approach everything with caution.

CHAPTER 5

Code Optimization

IN THIS CHAPTER

➢ Effective writing of code

➢ Error handling

➢ Security of code

In the last section, we learnt how to use Node.js to create an application that is based on the Internet of Things. Now in this chapter, we will look at Node's efficiency and performance in this chapter. We will concentrate on caching, load balancing, and monitoring the application.

JavaScript is the only programming language that springs to mind when it comes to designing a web application. Because it is simple to learn, it is the most popular programming language for web app development, works well with other languages, and can be used to create a wide range of applications. However, according to recent trends and surveys, Node.js is not only starting a new trend but also capturing all of the momentum in backend programming.

Businesses are aggressively looking for tools, technologies, and frameworks that enable them to maintain a strong grasp on numerous operating platforms with a single solution as the market becomes more competitive. Furthermore, many organizations believe Node.js to be an ideal alternative for server-side development in order to address the ongoing demand for apps that function smoothly and successfully across all platforms.

DOI: 10.1201/9781003357469-5

Because Node.js is highly stable and reliable JavaScript framework, large companies with high traffic, such as eBay, Microsoft, Yahoo, Netflix, and LinkedIn, are eager to hire Node.js app developers. Performance is critical when it comes to designing websites and applications. We need to know how long were users using our app, how frequently they depart, and how long it takes them to answer. The first 10 s are crucial in determining whether a person will abandon We're website or continue to interact with it. Obviously, we must speed up the website, deliver value inside the first 10 s, and attract the consumer to stay longer on web page. Although Node.js has numerous advantages, we should be aware of the complexity of the Node.js ticking machinery. We will talk about performance difficulties with Node.js here.

WHAT MAKES NODE.JS PERFORMANCE SO SPECIAL?

Google's V8, one of the fastest JavaScript engines available, powers Node.js.

Run-to-Completion, Single-Threaded Behavior

Let us have a look at the concept of single threading. Threading enables for parallel processing within an application, but Node.js does not have this capability. Alternatively, we can use asynchronous code and an event loop to create multi-tasking applications.

Detecting Memory Leaks

If a program is allocated some memory in RAM and not cleared after its action, the objects in the heap pile up continually until the working memory resource is exhausted, resulting in a crash, as we mentioned in a previous blog "Memory Leaks in Java." Although the garbage collector clears all the working memory, memory leaks are likely to occur in our applications. As a result, it's critical to keep a close eye on things and set up some alarming or warning features in the system.

We can dump the expose it to JavaScript using the V8 engine.

To address the limitations of it, the V8 engine uses two types of garbage collection.

- Mark sweep: slower than scavenge, but clears the working memory of all junk.

- Scavenge: quick, but doesn't remove all unreferenced items. In other words, it's unfinished.

We can collect debugging performance data and work on JavaScript performance optimization with Node.js profile via JavaScript utilizing V8 profiler.

WHAT IS AN EVENT LOOP AND HOW DOES IT WORK?

The event loop is a technique for breaking down long-running operations into manageable chunks. It can be used as an alternative to threading. The technique is similar to pulsation; Node.js scans the work queue and launches new tasks in milliseconds. If any work is required, Node.js directs them to the call stack and completes the task. The event loop allows Node.js to multitask, which means that additional tasks can begin without having to wait for the first one to finish.

THE EVENT LOOP AND NODE.JS PERFORMANCE

To avoid long-running synchronous operations like writing files, making network queries, and performing large calculations, it's crucial to understand Node.js' single-threaded nature. Let us look at an example: We want to create a Node.js application with two endpoints: one for file uploads and the other for searching user profiles.

The user profile fetching API will be used more frequently than the file uploading endpoint in general. If it does not react sooner than predicted, it will continue to prevent all users from loading the page. Users anticipate the file uploading API to take some time, but they won't be happy with slow page loads. If we don't use the event loop process when writing our Node.js program, Node.js may monopolize the user profile API while the users interact with the file upload API.

Setting Up, Running, and Analyzing a Performance Test for Node.js Application

We'll now learn how to set up, execute, and analyze a performance test for your Node.js application step by step.

- Choosing a Node.js performance testing tool: There are a number of performance optimization tools for each that has its own merits and demerits. When it comes to testing the speed of Node.js across the network from the outside world, it doesn't matter if your performance testing tool is written in Node.js or not.

- Let us start with a simple performance testing tool: Artillery. It's written in the Node.js programming language.

- As we set up Artillery, it will make regular queries to your Node.js application.

- We can tell Artillery which endpoints to request, at what rate, and for how long, among other things.

Let us see a basic test configuration.

```
Config:
target: 'https://artillery.io'
phases:
- duration: 45
arrivalRate: 15
defaults:
headers:
x-my-service-auth: '987401838271002188298567'
scenarios:
- flow:
- get:
URL: "/docs"
```

We're telling the Artillery to request your endpoints for 45 s at a rate of 15, which is about equivalent to 15 visitors arriving at the URL.

Then run the following commands to conduct the test:

```
run We're config.yml with artillery
```

Creating a Performance Test Profile in Node.js

A performance test profile specifies how your performance test will execute.

For example, if we start an e-commerce website, we can expect steady customer activity throughout the day. Alternatively, if our application is for booking tickets, we will see a lot of traffic for a short period of time, that is, the ticket booking opening time.

As a result, our performance test environment should be similar. We can make as many test profiles as we want and run them in any order we want.

Duplicating Large-Scale Distributed Systems

When an application reaches a certain scale, the traffic levels might become extremely high and unpredictable. We may also test our Node.js application with the desired percentage of users, and if performance degradation is detected, we can revert to the prior execution, which is a typical traffic levels. The key benefit of this technique is that we can test on our actual production application, so we do not have to worry about the test results failing to match the real thing.

We'll need data to figure out why our program is taking so long to load. We need to assess our application using Node.js performance monitoring after we acquire the data.

Configuring Our Monitoring

All apps are good and competent at what they do need some type of monitoring. These monitoring tools provide us a better understanding of the important performance metrics of our application. Before doing a performance test, we should have a better sense of what performance benchmark application is required to fulfill. What are our SLAs and KPIs (key performance indicators)? Which critical measures can assist us in better understanding a performance issue?

- Running with an API: APIs come in a variety of price points and functionality. It's critical to select the most appropriate tool for the requirements. To examine the performance, we should have as much data as possible.

The following is a great place to start:

- Infrastructure data: We'll almost certainly need data from the host where our application runs. We can receive this data in a primitive version of our application which runs on the cloud. This information will include our host's CPU usage, memory usage, and connection information.

- Application monitoring: These tools reside within our application's code and are capable of recording information such as how functions are called/performed, what problems we raise, and so on.

- Aggregated logs: Aggregated logs make it simple to search for and visualize our logged data. We may graph and record the performance of each of our APIs.

Setting Up a Node.js Performance Test Environment

Cloud hosting may be the most efficient approach to set up a test infrastructure. To eliminate request delay and data skewing, cloud hosting assures that the test is executed on the same machine and in the same location each time.

Running Our Tests

After starting our command line configuration, we will get requests to our Node.js application in this phase. We can use the selected monitoring solutions to see if the event loop is working properly, if requests to Node.js are taking longer than expected, and if connections are timed out. Experimenting with performance tests for Node.js speed and performance with tools like Artillery and Retrace might help us discover performance regression.

How to Make Node.js Run Faster

Let us look at several various techniques to make Node.js run faster.

Techniques for improving JavaScript performance include:

Tooling for the Frontend

It's critical on the front end that whatever sent to the browser is as minimal as feasible. This includes pictures, JavaScript, and CSS files in particular. Module bundlers (e.g., webpack, Parcel, Rollup) and task runners are involved in the process that makes this possible (e.g., Gulp, Grunt, etc.).

Task Runners and Module Bundlers

Module bundlers are build tools that combine a group of modules and their dependencies into a single file or a collection of files. After that, the output of such minification can be used in production. The minification process varies based on the tool we use, but for the most part, we can utilize the ES6 revision of JavaScript's standardized format for code modules. Complex transformations are possible, such as shortening multicharacter variable names or adopting a shorter syntax that is comparable to the original code, as well as consolidating multiple JavaScript files into one to decrease network queries. This is also true for CSS minification; superfluous whitespace and comments are deleted to make it easier for the browser to interpret the code.

Modules and Preprocessors for CSS

When it comes to minification, CSS is no different when it comes to decreasing browser requests during page load. Variables, functions, and mix-ins are provided by CSS pre-processors like post-CSS, Sass, and LESS to make CSS code maintenance and reworking easier. They also combine all files into a single.css file, reducing the number of round trips the browser must make to deliver the file. Scoped CSS names can be changed to global unique names using modern Node.js technology, such as the aforementioned bundlers. It's now as simple as requiring or importing a CSS module into our component's local scope, just like any other JavaScript module.

Images

When sending code to the browser, we need also to think about images. In general, the lighter our photographs are, the better. Depending on the device, we may want to utilize compressed images or provide alternate images. Gatsby, for example, is driven by Node.js behind the scenes and includes a plethora of Node-powered plugins, some of which are explicitly designed to turn images at build time into smaller ones and provide them on demand.

HTTP/2 and SSL/TLS

We can utilize HTTP/2 in a Node.js application to make web browsing easier while reducing bandwidth usage. It is aimed at increasing performance and addressing concerns with HTTP/1.x.

HTTP/2 has the following features:

- **Compression of HTTP headers:** This removes superfluous headers and compels all HTTP headers to be sent compressed.

- **Multiplexing:** This allows numerous requests to simultaneously retrieve resources and response messages over a single TCP connection.

Multiplexing is used to reduce the amount of requests sent to the server. The time it takes to establish an HTTP connection is frequently more expensive than the time it takes to send the data. The transport layer security (TLS) and secure socket layer (SSL) protocols are required to use HTTP/2. The fundamental functionality of Node.js makes setting up an HTTP/2 server a breeze.

Using Caching

Caching is a popular method for improving app speed. On both the client and server sides, it occurs. The client-side caching is the process of temporarily storing HTML pages, CSS stylesheets, JS scripts, and multimedia assets. Client caches save money on data by keeping frequently used information on the browser or on a content delivery network (CDN). Client caching occurs when a browser caches frequently requested data locally or on a CDN. The idea is that if a user visits a website and then leaves, the website should not have to download all of its resources again.

This is made feasible through HTTP cache headers. Cache headers are divided into two categories.

- The expiration date indicates when the resource must be requested again.

- Cache control: The max age indicates how long the resource is valid for.

Unless and until the resource has a cache header, the browser can only re-request the resource after the cache expiration date has elapsed. This method has some disadvantages. What happens, for example, if a resource is changed? The cache must be broken in some way. By addition of a version number to the resource URL, we can solve the issue using the cache-busting method. The resource is redownloaded when the URL changes. With Node.js technology like web pack, this is simple. Even if client-side caching is enabled, the app server will still need to render data for each different user using the app; hence, server-side caching must be implemented. Redis can be used with Node.js to store temporary data, which is known as object caching. To improve performance, we can usually combine client-side and server-side caching.

Caching is a great approach to improve our app's performance. If we have a limited number of users, our app's performance may not be affected. However, when traffic develops and load balance must be maintained, performance issues may arise. When this happens, caching our app on a regular basis will be a terrific way to improve performance. Caching can be difficult, so we'll need tools to help; we cache our app effectively, such as:

- Redis cache is designed to process cached data requests in a single thread and is completely asynchronous. Consider giving it a try. It's an easy-to-use API for managing our client-side and server-side cache.

- Mem cached is a distributed memory system that saves data over several nodes. It makes use of a hashing schema with hash table capabilities. These make sure that adding or removing a server node has no effect on the key-server node mapping.

- Node-set, cache's get, and delete methods are nearly equivalent to Mem cached's. It has a timeout that deletes data from the cache when the timeout period expires.

- Nginx will aid in load balancing. Nginx will aid in the caching of static files, allowing the application server to focus on other tasks. It has a minimal memory footprint and a high concurrency.

Improving Data Management Techniques

Optimization is crucial to performance since it streamlines system procedures and enhances overall app efficiency. We might be wondering what can be optimized in a Node.js application. Start by looking at how data is managed. Node.js programs may become slow due to a CPU/IO-bound job, such as a database query or a slow API request. In most Node.js projects, data is retrieved by sending an API request and returning a response.

WHAT IS THE MOST EFFICIENT WAY TO ACHIEVE THIS?

Pagination is a common approach that divides responses into batches of content that may be viewed using specific response queries. Pagination can be used to optimize the response while also preserving the larger quantity of data supplied to the user client.

Filtering is a useful strategy, as it allows the client to limit the results based on his or her own criteria. This will reduce the overall number of calls and the number of results displayed, but it also allows users to more precisely determine whether resources are offered depending on their needs. In REST API design, these two principles are frequently used.

Data is fetched in two ways such as underfetching and overfetching.

It offers more data than the client requires, whereas the latter fails to supply necessary data, necessitating a subsequent call to a different endpoint to finish the data collection. These two issues can arise on the client side as a result of insufficient app scaling. GraphQL is the situation because the server does not have to guess what the client wants; the client specifies their request and receives exactly what they want.

Load Balancing

It's a typical challenge to create high-performance apps that can handle a huge number of connections. To maintain the connections, one frequent option is to distribute traffic. Load balancing is a term for this method. To manage multiple connections, Node.js allows us to clone an application instance. This can be done with a single multicore server or several servers. The introduced cluster module can be used to scale a Node.js app on a multicore server by spawning new processes called workers (one for each CPU core) that all operate at the same time and connect to a single master process, allowing the processes to share the same server port. It acts as a single large multithreaded Node.js server. We can use the cluster module to allow load balancing and distribute incoming connections across all workers in an environment's numerous CPU cores using a round-robin technique.

Using the PM2 process manager to keep apps alive indefinitely is another option. This prevents downtime by restarting the app whenever a code update or error occurs. PM2 includes a cluster feature that allows us to run numerous processes over all cores without having to worry about modifying the code to use the native cluster module. Single-cluster design has downsides; we should plan to go from a single-server architecture to a multi-server architecture with reverse proxy-load balancing.

It (NGINX) allows load balancing over several Node.js servers, as well as a variety of load balancing strategies, such as:

- **Round robin:** A new request is routed to the next server in the list.

- **Least connections:** A new request is routed to the server with the fewest active connections.

- **IP hash:** A new request is sent to the server with the client's IP address hashed.

When employing several application servers, the proxy feature protects the Node.js server from direct internet traffic and allows us a lot of freedom.

Client-Side Authentication That Is Secure

If you want to provide users with a tailored experience, most web apps must preserve the state. If users can log in to our site, we'll need to keep track of their sessions.

We would normally produce a random session identifier to keep the session details on the server when implementing stateful authentication. We can use a central storage solution like Redis to store session data or the IP hash approach (in load balancing) to ensure that the user always reaches the same web server when scaling a stateful solution to a load-balanced application over numerous servers. There are some disadvantages to taking such a stateful strategy. Limiting users to a single server, for example, can cause problems if that server requires repair.

Another scalable approach, stateless authentication with JWT, is probably better. The benefit is always accessible, no matter which system is servicing a user. When a user logs in, a typical JWT implementation generates a token. The token is a base64 encoding of a JSON object that contains the required user information. The client gets the token, which is used to authenticate all API requests.

Maintaining a Lightweight and Compact Code

Make sure we use the principle of keeping our codebase minimal and concise while designing mobile and web apps. This is applicable for both the client and server code. Latency and load times will be reduced as a result. A one-page web app is a terrific option to consider when it comes to keeping our code short. Let us say our web app has a page with six JavaScript files on it. When we visit this website in our browser, it will make six HTTP calls to get all of our files. This will result in a blocking and waiting situation. There is an excellent illustration of how we may combine and connect numerous files into one to avoid situations like this.

There are numerous open-source libraries and modules for Node.js. During the development stage, we should consider why we are utilizing this framework rather than another. We must choose whether a framework is worthwhile to use or whether there are other, more straightforward ways to construct our code. The point is that using a framework should be well worth our time. This isn't to say that picking frameworks is a terrible idea. Frameworks are wonderful. They are scalable and have undeniable advantages. Only use a framework if it will make our code easier to understand.

Effective Server Communication with WebSockets

The HTTP request/response model has long been the foundation of the Internet. In online applications, WebSockets are an alternative to HTTP communication. They enable the client and server to communicate bi-directionally and long term. Once a channel is established, it remains open, allowing the client and server to communicate quickly and reliably. Both parties can start sending data at any time with minimal delay and overhead.

HTTP is efficient for data sharing and client-driven communication with limited user involvement. With WebSockets, a server can pass a message to a client without the client making an explicit request, allowing them to converse at the same time. This is ideal for in-the-moment and long-term communication. Ws is a well-known Node.js package for creating a WebSockets server. On the front end, JavaScript is used to connect to a WebSockets-enabled server and listen for events. Maintaining a large number of connections open at the same time demands a high-competition architecture with low-performance costs, which WebSockets provides.

Coding That Is Asynchronous

Single-thread concurrency architectures are used in Node.js. To provide a nonblocking operating flow, Node.js makes extensive use of asynchronous code. Other processing can proceed even before the first transmission is completed thanks to asynchronous I/O. Synchronous coding has the ability to make our website inaccessible. It employs blocking operations that may cause our main thread to become blocked, resulting in a significant reduction in web page speed. We can utilize queues to monitor our workflow with asynchronous code, allowing us to attach additional jobs and add extra callbacks without halting our main thread. Even if we strive to use asynchronous methods, it's possible that our web page will make blocking calls in some cases. When using third-party modules, this is a regular occurrence. Keep an eye on the external libraries we're utilizing and take steps to prevent them from dominating synchronous calls.

Take a look at the following example:

Using the Node.js file system, we used the file read operation in both models.

Synchronous

```
const fs = require('fs');
const content = fs.readFileSync("app.txt", "utf8");
console.log(content);
console.log('waiting for the file to read.........');
```

Asynchronous

```
//include file system module
const fs = require('fs');
//readFile() reads the file
fs.readFile("app.txt", "utf8", function (err, content)
{
    if (err) {
        return console.log(err);
    }
    //read the file
    console.log(content);
});
console.log('waiting for the file to read.....');
```

All operations are suspended until the synchronous fragment completes the data processing. Before printing the data and message to the console, readFileSync() will read the file and store its data in memory.

The console message will be printed asynchronously as the system does other activities. Even though it was the last command, "waiting for the file to read" is printed before the file content. When the file is read, a callback function will be called. Our application will run faster using the asynchronous approach, and we will avoid the so-called Call-back Hell.

Query Augmentation

Consider having a database table with over one million rows of data to query. The procedure generated by this database to obtain the data's endpoint will have a significant impact on the performance of our application. Bad queries will slow down our application, leaving our users frustrated. Query optimization is the solution to this problem.

OVERVIEW OF BASIC STRATEGIES FOR IMPROVING DATABASE PERFORMANCE/OPTIMIZATION

SELECT Should Be Avoided at All Costs

This would seem to be the most apparent way to choose our columns, right? However, we should keep in mind how time-consuming this question might be. Use a more separate technique to query columns in a table. Use the SELECT statement to query exactly the data we require, avoiding additional database fetching loads. Consider a table called Customers, which contains the fields FirstName, LastName, City, State, Zip, PhoneNumber, and Notes. The following two queries can be used to SELECT fields FirstName, LastName, City, State, and Zip.

First query

```
SELECT *
FROM Customers
```

Second query

```
SELECT FirstName, LastName, Address, City, State, Zip
FROM Customers
```

Even though we don't require all of the fields in this database, the initial query will pull them all. Because the second query will only return the required fields, it will be the more efficient approach to execute the SELECT statement. When using the INSERT and UPDATE commands, the same principle should be applied.

Use the WHERE Clause

The query's purpose is to retrieve the relevant records from We're database. The WHERE clause aids in record filtering and restricts the number of records pulled based on constraints. The WHERE clause takes the role of the HAVING clause, which chooses records prior to filtering the dataset. WHERE statements in SQL are faster because they reduce the amount of data that the database engine has to process.

To Sample the Query Results, Use LIMIT

Only the specified number of records will be returned by LIMIT. When using LIMIT to enforce a limit on a dataset, be sure the results are desirable and relevant. For example, if our Customer table has 500 records and we only require the first 100, LIMIT is an efficient technique to sample out the desired results while avoiding the selection of the remaining 400 records. Here's an illustration:

```
SELECT FirstName, LastName, Address, City, State, Zip
FROM Customers LIMIT 100
```

Avoid CHOOSE A UNIQUE OPTION
SELECT DISTINCT eliminates duplicate records by GROUPing them to produce unique results. Customers are shown in our table as an example.

```
SELECT DISTINCT Name, Surname, State, Zip FROM
Customers
```

Some common name and surnames, such as Johnny Depp, may be grouped together. As a result, the number of records will be incorrect. When a table contains a high number of customers with the name "David Smith," this query may take a long time to run. Use a more precise and efficient query such as:

```
SELECT FirstName, LastName, State, Zip FROM Customers
```

The number of records will be correct, as well.

Use the Wildcard (Percent) Character as Needed

If we want to SELECT consumers with first names that begin with the letter "Avi,"
First **query**

```
SELECT FirstName from Customers where FirstName like
'%avi%'
```

Second **query 2**

```
SELECT FirstName from Customers where FirstName like
'avi%'
```

FirstNames such as Avishek, Avinash, or Avik will be retrieved in the first query. This approach is inefficient since it may return unexpected results, such as David, Xavier, or Davin, if the FirstNames contains the letter "Avi." This wildcard may be performed more efficiently using the second query.

Using Off-Peak Hours to Run Queries

When the number of concurrent users is at its lowest, analytical and database management queries should be run in the production database; usually between the hours of 3 a.m. and 5 a.m.

Check out this article about MySQL query performance enhancement. It contains important MySQL hints that will help us improve our query writing skills.

GO WITHOUT A SESSION

Session information is saved in memory. As our app's traffic rises, more sessions will be produced, potentially causing substantial server burden. We must either find a way to save session data or find a way to reduce the quantity of data kept in a session. Stateless server protocols can be created with the help of modules like Express.js. Stateless protocols don't save or store data from earlier visits. Use an external session store like Redis, Nginx, or MongoDB instead. For improved speed, it's advisable to avoid storing session state on the server wherever possible.

Tracing and Logging of Scripts

We can use logging to keep track of the activities and traffic of our app. It is possible for fatal errors to occur while a program is executing (even though our app was running properly after production testing). We must receive this input quickly, determine which code contains the error(s), and correct them before our user sees a problem with our system.

Console.log(), which logs Standard outputs (stdout), and console.error() are two often used logging methods in Node.js (). They'll keep track of common errors. There are, however, more efficient and scalable libraries/third-party APIs for logging Node.js scripts.

They are as follows:

Winston

Winston is a simple, ubiquitous, and incredibly versatile multitransport async logger. It improves the flexibility and extensibility of logging. According to NPM statistics, it is the most popular logger. Winston has several transporters, each with a distinct default level of message priority.

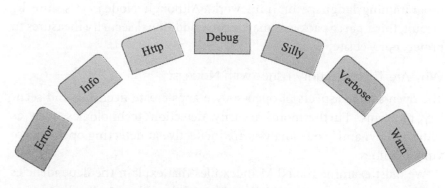

Several transporters levels of Winston.

Morgan

It is a middleware for Node.js applications that logs HTTP requests. Morgan provides insight into how our app is being used, as well as warnings about potential mistakes and concerns that may pose a threat to our app. Morgan is the most trusted HTTP logger among Node.js developers. Morgan is meant to log failures to the access-log or error log in the same way that servers like Apache and Nginx do.[1]

Bunyan

Bunyan is a simple logger that saves log entries in JSON format. The more detail regarding the code can be accessed from the page.[2]

Parallelism

When requesting remote services, database calls, or file system access, ensure parallel execution flow. Task parallelization reduces latency and eliminates any blocking procedures. The term "parallel operation" refers to the simultaneous execution of many tasks. Because our code will be tuned to run tasks at the same time, we won't be able to control which task finishes first. In most cases, Node.js does not do these several activities at the same time. Each task is then thrown into an asynchronous event loop, with no way of knowing which task will complete first. Consider using asynchronous execution if one or more tasks must be completed before the others.

NODE.JS ENCRYPTION GUIDELINES

Node.js is vulnerable to all forms of web app attacks, just like any other programming language or framework. Although Node.js is secure by default, third-party packages may require additional security measures to protect our website.

Why Are There Security Issues with Node.js?

The open-source aspects of open-source apps create licensing and security problems. Furthermore, security detection technologies such as static and dynamic code analysis are ineffective at detecting open-source vulnerabilities.

We must examine the NPM index files that explain the dependencies to find open-source parts in Node.js. Nonetheless, these index files do not contain any open-source parts that have been reused. Open-source projects are sometimes repurposed by the open-source community to reduce time-to-market, accelerate development, and add functionality. As a result, both commercial and open-source developers will be able to embed code snippets, functions, and approaches into files. In addition, many Node.js web development projects use terms other than the official Node.js license.

TOP NODE.JS SECURITY CONCERNS AND RECOMMENDATIONS

Because of Node.js' security weaknesses, we could be vulnerable to man-in-the-middle attacks, code injection, and sophisticated persistent threats. Here's a rundown of the Node.js security concerns that could lead to these flaws, as well as some potential solutions:

Validate User Inputs to Limit XSS Attacks

PROBLEM 5.1

Cross-site scripting, or XSS, allows hackers to inject vulnerable client-side scripts onto website pages that are viewed by many people. Data breaches can be caused via vulnerable client-side scripts. Furthermore, the hacker has access to the JavaScript code. Because user input is not vetted, this is the case. As a result, if something users put in the search field isn't discovered in the database, it will be returned to them in the same manner. As a result, a hacker can run a similar JS code by typing JS code into the search field instead of the product name.

SOLUTION

We can check the user's input. We can use output encoding methods or tools like the Jade engine with in-built encoding frameworks to prevent XSS attacks in Node.js. We can also use XSS-filters or Validator.js to accomplish this.

Data Leaks Should Be Avoided at All Costs

PROBLEM 5.2

Don't only rely on what the frontend gives us; additionally, consider what we'll provide it. We can easily transfer all of an object's information to the frontend and only show what we want. A hacker, on the other hand, can quickly detect the hidden data sent from the backend.

SOLUTION

Simply deliver the information that is needed. Simply pull the first and last names from the database if we only need them. This will require a bit more effort from We, but it will be well worth it.

Make Use of Security Linters

PROBLEM 5.3

Vulnerabilities can be scanned automatically. Additionally, we can detect basic security issues while writing the code.

SOLUTION

Linters such as eslint-plugin-security can be utilized as a solution. If we employ insecure programming, this type of security linter will alert us.

Each Request Should Have Access Control Implemented

PROBLEM 5.4

This is typically tied to the extent to which an app has been thoroughly assessed in terms of user permissions to specific URLs or areas within it. As a result, we can utilize access exposure to block areas of the application, such as the admin dashboard so that users without the proper role can access it at any time.

SOLUTION

The best method to eliminate this vulnerability is to manually test app modules that require certain user rights. To avoid the possibility of access rights being altered on the client side via JWT (JSON Web Token) authorization tokens or cookies, middlewares, and access control rules should be built on the server side.

Deserialization Using Encryption

PROBLEM 5.5

Deserialization and application of flawed objects via remote code implementation or API calls are examples of insecure deserialization. The CSRF (Cross-site Request Forgery) attack is the name for this type of attack. End users are forced to perform undesired actions on legitimate web apps as a result of this assault. Because the hacker cannot observe the falsified request reaction, CSRF attacks target changes in app state requests. Attackers can utilize social engineering techniques, such as distributing links via e-mail or chat, to lure victims into performing strange behaviors. CSRF can compel state-modifying requests, such as e-mail ID transformation and then fund transfer. For admin users, CSRF can compromise the entire web app.

SOLUTION

We must prevent CSRF attacks in order to reduce such hacks or attacks. Anti-forgery tokens in Node.js can be used to accomplish this. Anti-CSRF tokens are used to avoid one-click attacks as well as to check and validate the validity of user requests.

HTTP Response Headers Are Executed

PROBLEM 5.6

Express is one of the most widely used Node.js web app frameworks. Express, on the other hand, was not designed with security in mind. As a result, older Express versions could pose a security risk.

SOLUTION

To ensure the security of programs, we must utilize maintained and updated versions. In fact, by adding extra security-related HTTP headers to our app, we can prevent many less typical attacks. The most prevalent frameworks, such as CORS, can improve the security of our API, but consider using Helmet, which adds more headers to secure our project.

Helmet can be used to protect Express and Node.js applications. It's a set of middleware functions that, with a single line of code, run 11 different header-based security systems for We. It includes protection against cross-site scripting attacks, man-in-the-middle attacks, and secure server connection management.

Create a Logging and Monitoring System

PROBLEM 5.7

Security in Node.js also includes logging and monitoring. After all, our goal is to make mechanisms secure from the outset, but this necessitates a long-term process. We'll need logging and monitoring for this.

SOLUTION

Some hackers want to disable our program, which can be discovered without logging. However, some hackers choose to remain anonymous for a longer period of time. In this scenario, log and metrics monitoring will assist us in identifying the incorrect matter. We won't be able to tell if strange-looking requests are coming from our own app, a hacker, or a third-party API with just basic logging.

There are numerous tools, many of which talk to one another and combine to provide precise layers for strengthening the security of our system, which is dependent on data. Data is critical for assessing and recognizing potential app exposures and incursions. We can create a lot of routines that are based on a few predetermined system behaviors. Everything that happens inside an app is recorded and monitored. As a result, the monitoring acts as a warning voice that will attack us if something vulnerable is detected.

Authentication Should Be Strong and Thorough

PROBLEM 5.8

Another typical vulnerability is an authentication mechanism that is incomplete, weak, or malfunctioning. It's possible that this happens because many developers believe they're safe as is. Unstable or weak authentication, on the other hand, is easy to get around.

SOLUTION

One of the most effective options is to use current authentication solutions such as OAuth, Firebase Auth, or Okta. If we want to use Node.js authentication solutions, keep a few things in mind. When constructing passwords, never use Node.js' built-in crypto library; instead, use Scrypt or Bcrypt. Make sure that users are never alerted if their password or username is incorrect, and that failed login attempts are limited. We'll also need policies for dealing with sessions.

Scan Apps for Vulnerabilities on a Regular Basis

PROBLEM 5.9

In the Node.js ecosystem, we can install a variety of libraries and modules. Many of these can be used on a daily basis in our projects. As a result, a security risk exists. If we are using code written by someone else, we can't be sure it's secure.

SOLUTION

We must do automated vulnerability scanning on a regular basis to remedy this. This makes it easier to find dependencies that have similar faults. We can also utilize NPM analysis for easy monitoring; however, we should consider using tools like Retire.js, White Source Renovate, OWASP Dependency-Check, OSS INDEX, Acutinex, and NODEJSSCAN.

Build Pipelines for Security Patches Using Fluid

PROBLEM 5.10

Security misconfiguration vulnerabilities occur when web servers or apps are left unsecured or protected with insufficient security standards. Several aspects of the app stack (app containers, database, server, etc.) are vulnerable as a result of this flaw. Weak build pipelines are a common source of entry for security misconfiguration attacks, such as staging or development area credentials making it to creation. This exposes the app as staging or development area setups, resulting in lax security.

SOLUTION

It's best if we keep all three environments (development, staging, and production) the same with different credentials and access levels. Hackers can employ brute-force dictionary attacks against login forms with weak credentials if default package settings and user account passwords are used in Node.js apps. Default package settings, on the other hand, leave vulnerability pieces for malicious hackers.

GENERAL TIPS

Node.js is a popular lightweight JavaScript framework that lets us build sophisticated server-side and client-side apps. To get the most out of this application runtime environment, developers must write clean Node.js code, just like any other language.

Look at Our Naming Conventions

Checking how we name our JavaScript components, such as classes, functions, constants, and variables, is a fantastic place to start when producing clean and consistent Node.js code. Following a style guide whose coding standards and rules are widely accepted in the JavaScript community is the best strategy here. Use lowerCamelCase when naming functions and variables. Their names should be descriptive but not excessively long. Single-character variable names and uncommon abbreviations should be avoided.

```
// Wrong
function set_Price() {
}
// Correct
function setPrice() {
}
```

Use UpperCamelCase with the initial letter capitalized for class names, as seen below.

```
class SomeClassExample {}
```

We can use capital for the full word when naming constants, as seen below:

```
// Wrong
function set_Price() {
}
```

```
// Correct
function setPrice() {
}
```

We use an underscore to distinguish the names of constants and variables that have more than one name in the declaration.

```
var DAYS_UNTIL_TOMORROW = 1;
```

Where Functions Should Be Modularized

Creating a function for each activity is a simple method to declutter our code. If a function's name implies that it performs more than that, we should divide the functionality and create a new function. Our code will look cleaner if we keep smaller functional parts. We can also use the main `init()` function to save the application's structure. This allows us to reuse routines without having to write duplicate code. Functions that do a single activity are also easier to debug or modify because they don't need scanning the codebase for dependencies or figuring out which block of code performs a specific action.

Commenting in the Right Way

Comments are an important part of our Node.js code since they help to clarify tough sections and explain high-level techniques. They define the operation of a certain bit of code, allowing other programmers to better understand it. Avoid making superfluous remarks that repeat insignificant points when commenting. When creating comments, a good rule of thumb is to explain why we're doing something and leave the how-to to the code.

When Debugging, Be Aware of the Context

When it comes to software development, debugging is unavoidable, yet it's not always easy. When writing Node.js code, we have a lot of choices. For example, the console.log is a frequently used tool that allows us to troubleshoot our issues in a simple and rapid manner.

However, if we don't clean up the logs, our console may become a shambles. We should also consider implementing production debugging. The console will not provide us with enough information to determine the severity of an error in our live app. This isn't to say that we shouldn't use the console, but rather that we should use a tool that provides all of the debug info we'll need to figure out what's going on with our issues. Using a debugging tool like Raygun, we can find out what's wrong with our code.

Destructuring

Destructuring assignments is a fantastic technique for breaking down complicated data structures such as objects or arrays into smaller pieces. It allows us to quickly access array items and object properties.

Do Not Make the Same Mistake Twice

The final point involves the well-known DRY principle of software development, which uses data normalization and abstraction to remove repetition in program patterns. There are some of the tips that are required that fall under the category of coding style.

Callback Etiquette

An error-first callback interface should be exposed by modules.
    This is how it should be:

```
module.exports = function (dragonName, callback) {
  // do some stuff here
  var dragon = createDragon(dragon name);
  // The first parameter is the error
, which is null
in this case, but if an error happens, a new Error
 //should be supplied here.

  return callback(null, dragon);
}
```

ALWAYS DOUBLE-CHECK CALLBACKS FOR PROBLEMS

To further understand why this is required, start with an example that is broken in every way possible, then fix it.

```
/ This example is **BROKEN**; we'll repair it as soon
as possible:)
var fs = require('fs');
function readJSON(filePath, callback) {
  fs.readFile(filePath, function(err, data) {
    callback(JSON.parse(data));
```

```
  });
}
readJSON('./package.json', function (err, pkg) { ... }
```

The first issue with this readJSON function is that it never checks whether an error occurred during execution. Always keep an eye out for them.

Improved version is:

```
// this example is still broken, but we're working on
improving it!
function readJSON(filePath, callback) {
  fs.readFile(filePath, function(err, data) {
    // Here we check to see if there was an error
    if (err) {
      //transmit the error to the callback
  //keep in mind that error-first callbacks are
preferred.
      callback(err);
    }
    // no error, pass a null and the JSON
    callback(null, JSON.parse(data));
  });
}
```

On Callbacks, Return

One of the problems with the preceding example is that if an error occurs, the execution does not stop in the if statement, but rather continues. This can lead to a variety of unanticipated outcomes. Always return on callbacks, as a rule of thumb.

```
// This example is still broken, but we're working on
improving it!
function readJSON(filePath, callback) {
  fs.readFile(filePath, function(err, data) {
    if (err) {
      return callback(err);
    }
return callback(null, JSON.parse(data));
  });
}
```

Only Use Try-Catch in Sync Code

We're almost there! Another item to consider is the JSON.parse function. If JSON.parse is unable to convert the supplied string to a suitable JSON format, it will throw an exception. Because JSON.parse is synchronous, we may wrap it in a try-catch block. Please be aware that this can be done with synchronous code blocks; callbacks will not operate.

```
// this example **WORKS**! :)
function readJSON(filePath, callback) {
  fs.readFile(filePath, function(err, data) {
    var parsedJson;
    // Handle error
    if (err) {
      return callback(err);
    }
    // Parse JSON
    try {
      parsedJson = JSON.parse(data);
    } catch (exception) {
      return callback(exception);
    }
    // Everything is ok
    return callback(null, parsedJson);
  });
}
```

As Much as Possible Keep Away from It

Because Node requires a lot of callbacks and heavy usage of higher level functions to handle control flow, binding to a specific context is difficult. If we adopt a practical approach, we will save a lot of time and work. Of course, there are times when prototypes are more efficient, but try to avoid them if at all possible. Make a little module.

Do it in a Unix-like manner: Developers should create a software that is made up of basic elements connected by well-defined interfaces so that problems can be isolated and parts of the program may be altered in future versions to accommodate new features. Don't make Deathstars; keep it basic. A module should only perform one thing, and it should do it well.

Make Effective Use of Async Patterns

Use async

ERROR CORRECTION

Operational errors and programmer errors are the two basic types of errors.

Errors in Operations

Operational mistakes can occur in properly written applications as well, because they are caused by system/remote service issues, such as:

- system out of memory

- request timeout

- failed to connect to a remote service

Taking Care of Operational Errors

Depending on the sort of operational error, we can do one of the following:

- Try to fix the problem: If a file is missing, we might need to make one first.

- When dealing with network communication, retry the operation.

- Tell the client that something isn't right: useful when dealing with user inputs.

- When an error state is unlikely to alter on its own, such as when a program cannot read its configuration file, crash the process.

Errors in Programming

Errors in programming are known as bugs. This is something we should avoid, such as:

Referred to as an Async

Asynchrony refers to occurrences that occur outside of the principal program flow and strategies for coping with them in software programming. This category includes external events such as signals or activities triggered by a program that occur at the same time as program execution without prompting the program to block and wait for results. Asynchronous input/output is a function that doesn't have a callback and can't read undefined properties.

Taking Care of Programmer Faults

Because these issues are bugs, we won't know what condition our application is in until it crashes. When this happens, a process control system, such as supervisord or monit, should restart the application.

SUMMARY

In this section, we looked at how Node.js affects frontend tools, how HTTP/2 enhances Node.js performance, specialized caching solutions, and data handling approaches for improving Node.js performance. Then, we talked about how to manage multiple connections using load balancing in a Node.js project, the difference between stateful and stateless client-side authentication, and how WebSockets may provide a reliable connection between client and server. Now we have all we need to take advantage of Node.js' performance features and create applications that our consumers will enjoy. Performance optimization in Node.js is a large topic with a lot of areas to cover. Some of the popular methods can help us to get higher performance results:

- Using the most recent stable version Updates to Node.js.

- Tasks can be scheduled using Node.js timers.

- Access to local variables should be prioritized.

- Remove any.js libraries that are no longer in use.

- Delete any lines of code that are no longer in use.

- Avoiding global variables by having a well-defined execution context.

However, don't forget about security practices like SSL/TLS and HTTP/2, while we implement these optimization techniques. Because Node.js modules and frameworks enable app developers and engineers to design complex and unique systems, they also expose those systems to numerous security flaws. App developers will be able to construct more secure solutions for users if they stay on top of recent Node.js security practices. Clean, comprehensible code also aids in the creation of a firm foundation for readily maintainable programs.

NOTES

1. Morgan-npm.
2. Node-Bunyan-Trent.

CHAPTER 6

Summary

IN THIS CHAPTER

➢ Using Node.js with other frameworks and tools

➢ Node.js with React

➢ Node.js and Angular

The previous chapter taught us about code optimization, security, and general node advice. Now in this chapter, we will be learning all about the career prospects and the other frameworks that can be used along with node.js to design various applications.

CAREER PROSPECTS OF NODE.JS

Node.js is a software development technique that may be used to solve a variety of problems with servers and web applications. It is one of the most extensively utilized and well-known technologies. Node.js is an open-source and free programming language that runs on a variety of platforms including Windows, Linux, and Unix.

Some of the specifics of node.js are detailed below for a deeper and more in-depth understanding of this technology and its importance.

- To generate dynamic website content on the fly, Node.js is employed.

- Node.js is also used on the server to create, open, read, write, delete, and close files.

DOI: 10.1201/9781003357469-6

- Form data can also be collected using Node.js.

- Node.js allows us to add, delete, and modify data in a database.

- Node.js eliminates the need for waiting and streamlines the process by allowing us to focus on the next request.

- Single-threaded and nonblocking programming, both of which are asynchronous programming, can be run with Node.js. It has a high memory efficiency.

Most people begin their careers as frontend developers, creating applications using HTML, JavaScript, and CSS. Additional technologies must then be introduced into the project and node to make things more powerful and convenient. One such technique is js. App development, game development, and product creation are all possible job paths for Node.js experts.

Jobs as a software developer are always in high demand. All of these subareas, including frontend development, UX/UI development, server management, and backend development, require a highly experienced and skilled team. In terms of offered career positions as well as income in software engineering and node, full-stack development is the new segment that continues to lead the industry. JavaScript is a skill that makes a significant contribution. People earn substantial rewards in terms of wage raises, promotions, and professional progress after investing a significant amount of time and gaining sufficient authority over the subject.

Here are some interesting facts about Node.js that will make us want to study it:

- Demand that is persistent

The popularity of Node.js has been steadily increasing. In fact, Node.js has surpassed Java in popularity (the most popular programming language so far).

- There are more job opportunities in Node.js development

Companies are adopting Node.js for a variety of reasons, including reduced development time, lower server requirements, and unrivalled scalability. It is used by companies such as LinkedIn because it has greatly decreased their development time, and it has improved the load time of Netflix's application by 70%. Medium, The New York Times, PayPal, and other well-known companies in the tech industry employ Node.js. Startups are gradually catching up to this trend, adding Node.js into their technology stack. The benefits of Node.js are mostly due to its nonblocking event loop property, which allows it to quickly manage high numbers of requests, allowing for greater scalability.

- JavaScript is widely utilised

The best thing about Node.js is that it works with JavaScript. JavaScript is the most popular and easiest approach to creating web applications. JavaScript with an extra programming language such as PHP, Ruby, Python, and others are typically required to construct browser and server-side applications. We may use JavaScript to create both browser and server-side apps with Node.js. As a result, we'll need to learn JavaScript but no other server-side programming languages. In comparison to other languages and their event-loop systems, such as Python and Ruby, JavaScript outperforms them. Furthermore, because programmers may avoid mental switching between browser and server, there is less possibility for human error.

- In the quickest period possible, become a Full Stack Developer

To become a full-stack developer, we must understand both the frontend and the backend. Previously, in addition to JavaScript, one needed to know a server-side programming language. With Node.js, however, JavaScript may be used as a server-side programming language. We can start working as a full-stack developer using Express.js, Angular, and other frameworks.

- Salary packages that are attractive

The pay for Node.js developers is higher than for other technologies. Developers who are just starting out with Node.js should expect to earn between 5 and 10 LPA. This is largely dependent on a developer's skill level. Overall, with increased demand for Node.js, Node.js development is a viable employment prospect for both new and seasoned web developers wishing to advance their careers.

USING NODE.JS WITH OTHER FRAMEWORKS AND TOOLS

By employing a framework that incorporates fundamental application architecture, template engines, and integrated libraries, we can construct scalable, high-performance websites and apps with Node.js. They facilitate and speed up the development of server-side web applications. A Node.js framework holds placeholder pieces in an abstract design. To create a complete web application, we simply need to type in our own code. It looks after the rest of the app's structure. They also assist developers in defining the web app's control and data flows.

WHAT ARE THE ADVANTAGES OF UTILIZING NODE.JS FRAMEWORKS?

Node.js has a lot of built-in features that can be difficult to focus on if we aren't an expert. Sails and Express, for example, are Node.js frameworks that help us streamline our development process while taking care of the background complexities. Rapid development, better productivity, and, most crucially, seamless testing and debugging are all aided by this. They provide tools and plugins that make prototyping and developing apps easier. Web applications' performance and scalability are also improved by Node.js frameworks.

JS Frameworks and Their Types

- **Full stack:** Full-stack MVC frameworks provide developers with a one-stop shop. They include project scaffolding, in-built template engines, web socket support, and core UI libraries, among other things. Full-stack node JS frameworks can be used to create real-time, scalable web apps. Only JavaScript is used to control the back-end and frontend.

- **Microframeworks:** They are small frameworks that are used to accomplish a specific development goal. They are more versatile and give more configuration options than full-stack frameworks, and they are less opinionated.

- **Rest API frameworks:** These are server-side frameworks that are designed primarily for building powerful APIs. On our server, we can create a simple REST API to handle CRUD (Create-Read-Update-and-Delete) queries.

FRAMEWORKS FOR WEB APP DEVELOPMENT USING NODE.JS

There are several frameworks, some of which includes:

- **Express.JS:** Express.js is used to create backend services such as web sockets, web APIs, and other internet services. It's free and open-source software distributed under the MIT license, and it's based on the Sinatra micro-framework.

The Express.JS framework has the following important features:

- Express is a Node.js layer that provides online application development tools like basic routing, middleware, template engine, and static file serving on top of Node.js.

- It is simple and does not put a strain on Node.js performance. It is used to create modern online apps and web APIs.

- For code segmentation, Express leverages the Model-View-Controller (MVC) structure.

- Flexible and adaptable to individual requirements.

- Sets up middleware to handle HTTP requests and responses.

- A cutting-edge Object Relational Mapping (ORM) program that enables us to do costly CRUD operations.

- Uber, PayPal, IBM, and more firms use Express.js for server development.

- **Meteor:** It is a free and open-source framework for creating and deploying JavaScript web, desktop, and mobile apps. This framework is used for Node.js quick prototyping.

  Other benefits of using Meteor include:

- We may create a single source code that works across all platforms, including the web, desktop, iOS, and Android.

- The relational database MongoDB can be used with Meteor.

- Js is a programming language that aids with data synchronization.

- Meteor has a built-in capability called Live Reload that allows us to see our code logic without having to recompile the project or refresh the browser page.

- Meteor includes a platform for developing reactive user interfaces.

- A single language is utilized continuously across the application, which improves consistency.

- The webpage can be updated in real-time.

- **Sail:** Sails is a JavaScript framework with an MVC design built on top of Node JS. It is the best option for designing enterprise apps and online APIs in a straightforward and straightforward manner. More data requests, automatic production of JavaScript Object Notation (JSON) requests, and extra HTTP capabilities are all part of Sails' upgraded Rails version of MVC software design.

  - Waterline, a strong ORM included with Sails, provides a simple data access layer for any popular database.

  - Sails has blueprints and scaffoldings that we can use to get our app's backend up and running quickly and without coding.

  - Web sockets are supported by every route in our Sails app, and they will translate incoming socket messages.

- **Nest.js:** Nest.js, one of the most forward-thinking Node js frameworks, is used to create dynamic and scalable enterprise and business applications. With a large library selection, it provides complete flexibility to developers like us. Nest's primary programming languages are progressive JavaScript and TypeScript.

  - Nest is ensured because Typescript is enabled. Js features a solid typing system and follows excellent coding guidelines.

  - It is a multiparadigm framework that implements principles such as OOP (Object Oriented Programming), FP (Functional Programming), and FRP (Functional Reactive Programming).

  - It comes with a productivity accelerator on the backend. It offers a highly extensible ecosystem that allows for the creation of full-featured server-side applications.

  - The Nest CLI is a powerful tool that allows us to create several prebuilt features for our web application.

- **Koa:** The Express.js team created Koa, a highly extendable minimalist web framework for Node.js. A Koa web application resembles an object with a collection of middleware functions. When a user asks something, Koa puts these functions on a stack and performs them.

  - Even at the lowest middleware levels, high-level JavaScript improves compatibility and resilience.

- Provides content negotiation, cache freshness, proxy support, pop-ups, and redirection capabilities.

- It provides a framework for middleware that may be extended without being integrated into its core, resulting in a reduced footprint.

- The most crucial aspect is that we can work without having to wait for callbacks.

- **Hapi:** It's one of the safest and simplest Node.js frameworks, thanks to input validation. The Hapi.js framework has some major features, including:

  - Its architecture is plug-in-based.

  - Has a robust ecosystem with a plethora of security defaults.

  - PayPal Hapi framework delivers dynamic content for customers by quickly executing the JavaScript template engine, which is used by large-scale enterprises such as Disney.

  - It's quite scalable, and numerous third-party plugins are supported. These plugins make it possible to create real-time talking programs that can handle thousands of people.

  - It facilitates the creation of detailed papers for developers.

- **Derby:** It is a full-stack web framework for Node.js online application development. It's noted for its "Racer Engine support," which allows many users to work on the same data in real time. This Node framework uses Share DB's Operational Transformation services to use a sophisticated conflict resolution algorithm for offline access, real-time updates, and rapid interactions.

  - Derby.js combines server and client web browsers, allowing both backend and frontend code to be written in a single file.

  - Derby employs templates for data rendering; therefore, there's no need to create the costly DOM implementations on the server side.

  - Derby.js produces the HTML output of templates on the server for faster page loading.

- It provides complete assistance with search engine optimization.

- Derby.JS renders with fast, native DOM manipulation techniques on the client-side web browsers.

Loopback

LoopBack is a Node.js and TypeScript API MVC framework that allows us to quickly develop APIs and microservices made of backend systems. Loopback connects our API to its backend data sources in a seamless manner. When we send a data model description to LoopBack, which is built on top of Express, it will generate an end-to-end REST API.

- API explorer, an inbuilt client, allows us to dynamically explore our application.

- Creates data models from schemas using MySQL, MongoDB, and Oracle databases.

- For speed, SOAP or REST services are used.

- It includes a basic CLI that allows for quick and easy prototyping.

- It works with Android, iOS, and web browsers to support native mobile and browser development.

- Add-on components can be used for file management, third-party login, and more.

Adonis

It is a JavaScript MVC framework that supports the Express, Koa, and MEAN tech stacks internally. The PHP-based Laravel had a big influence on the developers, and they share a lot of similarities with it.

- Adonis.js offers a robust environment with many standard features incorporated into the framework's core.

- It is built on the MVC architecture and focuses on getting things done quickly using dependency injection and IOC ideas (inversion of control).

- Route groups, subdomain-based routing, and resource resources are all supported by AdonisJS' routing layer.

- This Node.js framework allows us to configure web sockets and includes built-in modules for Redis, e-mails, data validation, ORM, and authentication.

- Sessions, API tokens, and OAuth-based user login are all supported by a flexible authentication mechanism.

- Use the predefined authorization actions and policies to manage user access.

- A command-line interface (CLI) is included to let us develop custom commands and automate our workflows.

- It's simple to pick up and has a gradual learning curve.

Total

It is a modern, modular node framework that follows the MVC architectural pattern. Among the framework's unique characteristics are:

- A set of libraries and packages make up the Total Platform.

- It is incredibly quick and requires very little maintenance, thanks to the best development principles influenced by ASP.NET MVC and Django for web app development.

- Total Eshop, one of the greatest Node.js e-commerce systems, is included.

- PostgreSQL, MongoDB, CouchDB, Firebase, Redis, and more databases are all supported.

- The total.js platform is designed to be self-contained. We can construct web applications with Notepad or Nano code editors without needing any other tools or knowing new programming languages.

HOW DO WE PICK THE BEST FRAMEWORK FOR OUR WEB APPS?

Node.js is a flexible JavaScript tool that may be used to construct

- Apps that update in real-time

- Applications that stream data

- Apps for texting

- Apps for chatting

- Apps for social media

- Emulators in the virtual world

- Games with multiple players

- Collaboration software

- Minimum value products

IS NODE.JS COMPATIBLE WITH REACT?

Yes. Node.js allows us to create scalable and quick RESTful APIs on the backend. In contrast, React is a frontend framework for building interactive user interfaces. We can quickly create complex and scalable web apps using both tools.

Node is the most widely used platform for hosting and running React web servers. After all, the Node Package Manager (NPM) CLI allows us to install any package using NPM. Furthermore, Node compiles a React application into a single file using Webpack and other plugins.

WHY USE NODE.JS AND REACT TOGETHER FOR WEB APP DEVELOPMENT?

For web app development, there are unique reasons to leverage the lethal combo of Node.js and React. Here are a few examples:

- **The ability to scale:** Using Node and React together, developers can construct dynamic, massive, data-driven internet apps that are responsive across several devices. While working on significant projects and maintaining the performance of our website, having scalability would be advantageous.

- **MERN Stack no. 2:** MongoDB, Express, React, and Node.js make up the MERN Stack. And no greater combination than these frameworks may give a website a unique dimension. Along with React.js, MERN Stack supports Node.js. As a result, we may use the Node and React combination to create web apps.

- **APIs based on JSON:** Because of React.js' high code reusability and access to rapid code sharing, creating JSON APIs for web development is simple. And Node.js is up to the task.

- **APIs based on JSON:** Because of React.js' high code reusability and access to rapid code sharing, creating JSON APIs for web development is simple. This is something that Node.js is capable of.

- **Data in real time:** Because our business app requires a continuous server connection, we should utilize Node.js if it handles real-time data management or wants to construct a data streaming app.

- **Rapid progress:** We may get a great return on investment and save money and time by combining React and Node for web app development. After all, these technologies combine to provide a fantastic framework for creating fast-loading, easy-to-maintain websites.

- **Special purpose areas; single page applications:** Is our company in need of a single-page app with asynchronous data loading? Then, we should choose React with Node as our backend since it allows us to create a lightweight backend model using callback functions.

- **Code in the same language for the frontend and backend:** Developers can avoid learning difficult backend languages like Python or Ruby by combining Node and React. They can write server-side code with Node and frontend code with React without switching frameworks or programming languages.

- **There's a lot of traffic on our server:** When developers work on web app development, the combination of Node.js and React might help to balance heavy server requests and load.

- **Process management:** React and Node combine to provide a well-organized web development process. These technologies are, after all, scalable, efficient, and quick. They may assist us in creating high-functioning websites if we work with them together.

- **JavaScript is being used more often:** For frontend and back-end coding, Node with React allows us to access the full power of JavaScript. It allows us more flexibility and convenience when developing websites or web apps because we can use a single language for everything.

HOW TO CREATE AN ANGULAR APP USING NODE.JS

We can create Angular apps in a variety of methods and deploy them to production. One method is to create Angular using Node.js or Java, while another one is to create Angular and deliver static content using the NGINX web server. With Node.js, we must also deal with server code; for example, we must use node to load the index.html page.

Introduction

Angular is a JavaScript framework for developing online apps that does not require the browser to be open. We need a system that loads Angular's index.html (single page) in the browser together with all of its dependencies (CSS and JS files). The web server in this example is node, which loads Angular assets and takes API calls from the Angular app.

Prerequisites

For this post, there are a few prerequisites. We'll need node.js installed on our laptop, as well as an understanding of how HTTP works. We will need them on our laptop if we want to practice and run this on it.

- ngx-bootstrap

- Node.js

- Angular CLI

- Typescript

- VSCode

Project Exercising

This is a small project that shows how to create and operate an Angular application using Node.js. We have a simple software that allows us to add people, count them, display them on the side, and retrieve them at any time.

We make an API call to the node.js server to store users as we add them, and we obtain the same data from the server when we retrieve them. In the video below, we can watch network calls.

The GitHub page for this project may be found here. We can clone it and run it on our own machine.

```
// clone the project
https://github.com/bbachi/angular-Node.js-example.git
```

```
// install and start the project
npm install
npm start
```

Only a minimal bit of Node.js is required for this project.

If we're new to Node.js, don't worry; this brief description will get us up and running with this project. We can skip this section if we are already familiar with Node.js. For server-side applications, Node.js is an asynchronous event-driven JavaScript runtime environment. The most recent version of Node.js is 12, which we may download from this link. We can download the Node.js package and install it on our laptop by clicking on any LTS link. The command node -v can be used to determine the Node's version. By running the command node on the CLI, we can run JavaScript on the node REPL.

We've finished installing a node and learned how to use JavaScript. JavaScript files can also be run. Let's put the above commands in the sample.js file and run it with node sample.js.

```
var x = 10;
var y = 20;
var z = x + y;
console.log(z);
```

Phase of Development

Typically, the ways in which we create, build, and run in production are vastly different. As a result, I'd like to divide the process into two phases: development and production.

We operate the Node.js server and the Angular app on separate ports during the development period. It is easier and quicker to develop in this manner. The Angular app is running on port 4200 with the support of a Webpack dev server, and the Node.js server is running on port 3080, as shown in the diagram.

Structure of the Project

Let's have a look at the project structure for this one. There will be two packages available. There are two JSON files, one for Angular and the other for the Node.js API. It's always a good idea to have entirely separate node modules for each one. We won't have any merging issues or other issues with web and server node module collisions if we do it this way.

API for Node.js

On the server side, we utilize express and nodemon. Express is a Node.js web framework that is fast, unopinionated, and simple, and nodemon is a library that makes our API refresh automatically anytime the files change. Let's get these two dependencies installed. Install this as a dev dependent because nodemon is only used for development.

```
npm install express --save
npm install nodemon --save-dev
```

Here's the whole stuff. Node.js API's JSON

```json
{
  "name": "angular-Node.js-example",
  "version": "1.0.0",
  "description": "node server",
  "main": "index.js",
  "scripts": {
    "start": "node index.js",
    "dev": "nodemon ./server.js localhost 3080",
    "test": "echo \"Error: no test specified\" && exit 1"
  },
  "repository": {
    "type": "git",
    "url": "git+https://github.com/bbachi/angular-Node.js-example.git"
  },
  "author": "Bhargav Bachina",
  "license": "ISC",
  "bugs": {
    "url": "https://github.com/bbachi/angular-Node.js-example/issues"
  },
  "homepage": "https://github.com/bbachi/angular-Node.js-example#readme",
  "dependencies": {
    "express": "^4.17.1"
  },
  "devDependencies": {
    "nodemon": "^2.0.2"
  }
}
```

Import express and define two routes: /API/users and /API/user, as well as a server listening on port 3080. The server.js file may be found here. To handle data in the HTTP request object, we utilize body-parser.

```
const express = require('express');
const app = express(),
      bodyParser = require("body-parser");
      port = 3080;

const users = [];

app.use(bodyParser.json());

app.get('/api/users', (req, res) => {
  res.json(users);
});

app.post('/api/user', (req, res) => {
  const user = req.body.user;
  users.push(user);
  res.json("user addedd");
});

app.get('/', (req,res) => {
    res.send('App Works !!!!');
});

app.listen(port, () => {
    console.log('Server listening on the port:
:${port}');
});
```

When we use the command npm run demand to start the Node.js API, whatever file we alter will be automatically updated.

ANGULAR APPLICATION

The Node.js API is now accessible via port 3080. It's now time to have a peek at the Angular app. The folder my-app contains the complete Angular app. With the command ng new my-app, we can build a new app. I won't post all of the files here; instead, we can view them all at the above Github site or here.

Let's have a look at some key files. This is the service file that uses the node API.

```
import { Injectable } from '@angular/core';
import { HttpClient } from '@angular/common/http';

@Injectable({
  providedIn: 'root'
})
export class AppService {

  constructor(private http: HttpClient) { }

  rootURL = '/api';

  getUsers() {
    return this.http.get(this.rootURL + '/users');
  }

  addUser(user: any) {
    return this.http.post(this.rootURL + '/user',
{user});
  }

}
```

The app component that subscribes to these requests and retrieves data from the API is shown in the following code:

```
import { Component, OnDestroy } from '@angular/core';
import { FormGroup, FormControl, Validators } from '@
angular/forms;
import { AppService } from './app.service';
import { takeUntil } from 'rxjs/operators;
import { Subject } from 'rxjs';

@Component({
  selector: 'app-root',
  templateUrl: './app.component.html',
  styleUrls: ['./app.component.css']
})
```

```
export class AppComponent implements OnDestroy {

  constructor(private appService: AppService) {}

  title = 'angular-Node.js-example';

  userForm = new FormGroup({
    firstName: new FormControl('', Validators.
nullValidator && Validators.required),
    lastName: new FormControl('', Validators.
nullValidator && Validators.required),
    email: new FormControl('', Validators.
nullValidator && Validators.required)
  });

  users: any[] = [];
  userCount = 0;

  destroy$: Subject<boolean> = new Subject<boolean>();

  onSubmit() {
    this.appService.addUser(this.userForm.value).
pipe(takeUntil(this.destroy$)).subscribe(data => {
      console.log('message::::', data);
      this.userCount = this.userCount + 1;
      console.log(this.userCount);
      this.userForm.reset();
    });
  }

  getAllUsers() {
    this.appService.getUsers().pipe(takeUntil(this.
destroy$)).subscribe((users: any[]) => {
      this.users = users;
    });
  }

  ngOnDestroy() {
    this.destroy$.next(true);
    this.destroy$.unsubscribe();
  }
}
```

The Angular and Node APIs Work Together

The Angular app is running on port 4200 with the support of a webpack dev server and a Node.js API on port 3080 during development.

These two should be interacting in some way. All API calls can be proxied to the Node.js API. Angular has a proxying technique built-in. To begin, we must define the following proxy. conf.json is located in the my-app folder.

```
{
  "/api": {
    "target": "http://localhost:3080",
    "secure": false
  }
}
```

If we check at the file, we'll notice that all paths beginning with/API are redirected to http://localhost:3080, which is where the Node.js API is operating. The proxyConfig key must then be defined in angular.json under the serve portion.

```
// Node.js API (Terminal 1)
npm run dev
// Angular app (Terminal 2)
npm start
```

How to Create a Production-Ready Project

With the support of a webpack dev server, the Angular app runs on port 4200. When it comes to running in production, this is not the case. We must create the Angular project and use the node server to load the static assets. Let's take a look at them one by one.

First, we must build the Angular project using the command npm run build, which will place all of the produced assets in the dist folder.

- Second, we need to make some server-side adjustments. The changed server.js file may be found here.

- We need to use express.static to tell express that the Angular build has a dist folder and assets.

- load index.html for the default path.

```
const express = require('express');
const app = express(),
      bodyParser = require("body-parser");
      port = 3080;

const users = [];

app.use(bodyParser.json());
app.use(express.static(process.cwd()+"/my-app/dist/
angular-Node.js-example/"));

app.get('/api/users', (req, res) => {
  res.json(users);
});

app.post('/api/user', (req, res) => {
  const user = req.body.user;
  users.push(user);
  res.json("user addedd");
});

app.get('/', (req,res) => {
  res.sendFile(process.cwd()+"/my-app/dist/angular-
Node.js-example/index.html")
});

app.listen(port, () => {
    console.log('Server listening on the
port::${port}');
});
```

After we've made the above modifications, we may execute the entire project using the node.js server on port 3080, as shown below, because node.js also works as a web server.

SUMMARY

Node.js is an enterprise-grade framework for mobile app development that supports both server-side and client-side JavaScript. Despite the fact that Node.js frameworks aren't required for backend development, they improve development productivity, product performance, and code quality significantly. Developers can drastically speed up the development process if they have access to templates, libraries, modules, and middleware. They can manage hundreds of requests and callbacks and combine Node.js with client-side frameworks with ease.

Bibliography

1. Node.js Introduction – https://www.w3schools.com/nodejs/nodejs_intro.asp, accessed on July 15, 2022.
2. What Is Node.js – https://www.tutorialspoint.com/nodejs/nodejs_introduction.htm, accessed on July 15, 2022.
3. Node.js Application – https://nodejs.dev/en/learn/introduction-to-nodejs/, accessed on July 15, 2022.
4. JavaScript History – https://www.infoworld.com/article/3210589/what-is-nodejs-javascript-runtime-explained.html, accessed on July 15, 2022.
5. Why Node.js? – https://medium.com/free-code-camp/what-exactly-is-node-js-ae36e97449f5, accessed on July 15, 2022.
6. Fundamentals of Node.js – https://www.educative.io/blog/what-is-nodejs, accessed on July 15, 2022.
7. Node.js Basics – https://www.tutorialsteacher.com/nodejs/nodejs-basics, accessed on July 15, 2022.
8. Node js Data Types – https://www.etutorialspoint.com/index.php/nodejs/node-js-datatype, accessed on July 15, 2022.
9. Node.js Functions – https://www.simplilearn.com/tutorials/nodejs-tutorial/nodejs-functions, accessed on July 16, 2022.
10. Node.js String Functions – http://www.java2s.com/Tutorials/Javascript/Node.js_Tutorial/0050__Node.js_String_Functions.htm, accessed on July 16, 2022.
11. Node.js split() Function – https://www.geeksforgeeks.org/node-js-split-function/, accessed on July 16, 2022.
12. JavaScript Strings – https://www.tutorialsteacher.com/javascript/javascript-string, accessed on July 16, 2022.
13. How to Create a Web Server in Node.js with the HTTP Module – https://www.digitalocean.com/community/tutorials/how-to-create-a-web-server-in-node-js-with-the-http-module, accessed on July 16, 2022.
14. Environment Setup – https://www.tutorialspoint.com/nodejs/nodejs_environment_setup.htm, accessed on July 16, 2022.
15. Setting Up a Node Development Environment – https://developer.mozilla.org/en-US/docs/Learn/Server-side/Express_Nodejs/development_environment, accessed on July 17, 2022.
16. JavaScript Runtime Environments – https://www.codecademy.com/article/introduction-to-javascript-runtime-environments, accessed on July 17, 2022.

17. Five Ways to install Node.js – https://www.nodejsdesignpatterns.com/blog/5-ways-to-install-node-js/, accessed on July 17, 2022.
18. Overview of Node.js – https://en.wikipedia.org/wiki/Node.js, accessed on July 17, 2022.
19. Latest LTS Version: 18.14.0 – https://nodejs.org/en/download/, accessed on July 17, 2022.
20. Differences between Node.js and the Browser – https://nodejs.dev/en/learn/differences-between-nodejs-and-the-browser/, accessed on July 17, 2022.
21. Is Node.js Used for Frontend or Backend? – https://www.simplilearn.com/tutorials/nodejs-tutorial/nodejs-backend#:~:text=Frontend%20or%20Backend?-,Node.,as%20well%20as%20the%20backend, accessed on July 18, 2022.
22. Anna Dziuba – What Is Node.js Used for? – https://relevant.software/blog/why-and-when-to-use-node-js/#:~:text=Real-time%20applications.,users%20at%20the%20same%20time, accessed on July 18, 2022.
23. MVC Framework – Introduction – https://www.tutorialspoint.com/mvc_framework/mvc_framework_introduction.htm, accessed on July 18, 2022.
24. Four Frameworks of the Apocalypse – https://www.toptal.com/nodejs/nodejs-frameworks-comparison, accessed on July 18, 2022.
25. Kristopher Sandoval – Node.js Frameworks to Build Web APIs – https://nordicapis.com/13-node-js-frameworks-to-build-web-apis/, accessed on July 18, 2022.
26. What is Google Cloud Platform (GCP)? – https://www.edureka.co/blog/what-is-google-cloud-platform/, accessed on July 18, 2022.
27. Shailendra Chauhan – What Is Microsoft Azure? – https://www.dotnettricks.com/learn/azure/getting-started-with-microsoft-azure-platform, accessed on July 18, 2022.
28. Shyamli Jha – What Is Microsoft Azure: How Does It Work and Services – https://www.simplilearn.com/tutorials/azure-tutorial/what-is-azure, accessed on July 19, 2022.
29. Red Hat OpenShift Online – https://access.redhat.com/products/openshift-online-red-hat, accessed on July 19, 2022.
30. V8 JavaScript Engine – https://nodejs.dev/en/learn/the-v8-javascript-engine/, accessed on July 19, 2022.
31. Mahipal Nehra – Why Choose NodeJS for IoT Applications – https://www.decipherzone.com/blog-detail/nodejs-for-iot-applications#:~:text=The%20preliminary%20reason%20for%20NodeJS,machine%20code%20with%20faster%20execution, accessed on July 19, 2022.
32. Sandeep Pandah – Tips to Make Your Node.js Web App Faster – https://www.sitepoint.com/10-tips-make-node-js-web-app-faster/, accessed on July 19, 2022.
33. Roshan Kumar – Steps to Select the Right Database for Your Internet of Things System – https://thenewstack.io/4-steps-to-select-the-right-database-for-your-internet-of-things-system/, accessed on July 19, 2022.

34. Traci Ruether – What Is a CDN and Why Is It Critical to Live Streaming? – https://www.wowza.com/blog/cdn-live-streaming, accessed on July 19, 2022.
35. Why Is Node.js Single Threaded? – https://www.quora.com/Why-is-Node-js-single-threaded-Is-it-a-constraint-of-the-V8-engine-or-of-the-JavaScript-language-itself, accessed on July 19, 2022.
36. Why Use Node Js Development for IoT Applications? – https://evontech.com/component/easyblog/why-use-node-js-development-for-iot-applications-top-reasons.html?Itemid=159, accessed on July 19, 2022.
37. Sandeep Panda – Make Your Node.js Web App Faster – https://www.sitepoint.com/10-tips-make-node-js-web-app-faster/, accessed on July 19, 2022.
38. Build a Video Streaming Server with Node.js – https://blog.logrocket.com/build-video-streaming-server-node/, accessed on July 19, 2022.
39. Max Wilbert – Private Streaming Platforms for Live Stream Events – https://www.dacast.com/blog/7-live-streaming-solutions-for-private-events/, accessed on July 20, 2022.
40. Node.js Event Loop – https://www.geeksforgeeks.org/node-js-event-loop/, accessed on July 20, 2022.
41. Ben Lutkevich – CDN (content delivery network) – https://www.techtarget.com/searchnetworking/definition/CDN-content-delivery-network, accessed on July 20, 2022.
42. Open Source Security Explained – https://snyk.io/series/open-source-security/, accessed on July 20, 2022.
43. Hardik Shah – How to Make a Streaming App: Features, Tech Stack & Cost Analysis – https://www.simform.com/blog/how-to-make-a-streaming-app/, accessed on July 20, 2022.
44. How to Become a Full Stack Developer – https://bootcamp.cvn.columbia.edu/blog/how-to-become-a-full-stack-developer/, accessed on July 20, 2022.
45. Easy HTTP/2 Server with Node.js and Express.js – https://webapplog.com/http2-node/, accessed on July 20, 2022.
46. Oskar Petr – How to Create your First Modern Angular App with Node.js – https://javascript.plainenglish.io/how-to-create-your-first-modern-angular-app-with-node-js-b9824869cbfa?gi=5a8c5ad8f92, accessed on July 20, 2022.
47. Five Reasons to Choose Node.js for Web Development https://edwisor.medium.com/5-reasons-to-choose-node-js-for-web-development-747e5d8e2fd6, accessed on July 21, 2022.
48. The WebSocket API – https://developer.mozilla.org/en-US/docs/Web/API/WebSockets_API, accessed on July 21, 2022.
49. Mateusz Piguła – Socket.io tutorial: Real-Time Communication in Web Development – https://tsh.io/blog/socket-io-tutorial-real-time-communication/, accessed on July 21, 2022.
50. Martin Fietkiewicz – WebSockets vs. HTTP: Comparing Pros and Cons – https://ably.com/topic/websockets-vs-http, accessed on July 21, 2022.

Index